The Cry God Answers

Finding Restoration Through Intercession

Rosemarie Turminaro Brown

ISBN 0-9754897-6-3
Joshua Publishing
15941 W. 65th St. #177
Shawnee, KS 66217
1.877.626.7596
www.joshuapublishing.net
Email: service@joshua-publishing.com

Reviews for *The Cry God Answers*

"You are to be commended for the splendid truth and style in communicating the burden of your heart as God has revealed the subject matter to you. It is indeed fitting for the time and hour now facing the church and God's people. The Biblical analogies you show in representing God's mannerism of using His own people in secret closets of prayer is most encouraging and should help many in our day enter into this most important ministry for the sake of God's purpose and plan to change our world."

Rev. R. Stanley Berg, Retired Pastor
Glad Tidings Tabernacle, New York, New York

"Definitely distinctive, compassionately convicting, and powerfully provocative. The best book so far on the topic of restoration and intercession. It is a definitive description of the road to healing, restoration and revival. Truly a masterpiece and a work of art! One great book!"

Bishop Peter Bruno, Sr.
Nutley Abundant Life Worship Center, Nutley, New Jersey

"You have written a once a year book (It should be read once a year). This book holds the Word transmitted with insight, anointing, and practicality. All the tempted, tested and befuddled will find light at the end of the tunnel. That means, all of us. Thank you Rosemarie."

Rev. Aimee G. Cortese, Pastor
Crossroads Tabernacle, Bronx, New York

"I have been blessed and instructed by *The Cry God Answers*. Rosemarie Brown carefully explains a broader understanding of intercessory prayer that leads to restoration. She has provided a helpful guide to apply the biblical stories leading us to intercessory prayer for others as we face our own needs."

Dr. William Crothers, Former President
Roberts Wesleyan College, Rochester, New York

"What a powerful book! It is my pleasure and privilege to recommend *The Cry God Answers* to everyone...Readers will be blessed, challenged and changed."

Rev. Mary L. Edlin, Senior Pastor
Faith Temple, Rochester, New York

"*The Cry God Answers* is simple to read and strong in word which is an unbeatable combination when warmed by the Spirit. Thank you for your work of grace to the Body which so needs this kind of ministry. It ministered to my spirit and left me satisfied that all I knew all the time could still be trusted and tried. Your prescription is so pure, so practical and so very powerful. Thank you for sharing your head and your heart with us all. Do it again! and again."

Rev. Andrew G. Farina, Senior Pastor
Christian Assembly, Greenville, PA

"True intercession is primarily an expression of burden, not vision. The Holy Spirit';s promise is that He will pray through us with "groanings that cannot be uttered." My friend Rosemarie Brown, an intercessor herself, has captured the essence of prayer by examining scriptural characters as they faced overwhelming circumstances. This book is a must for anyone desiring to see their situation change and draw close to God. It is a work of art, orchestrated by the Spirit of God."

Rev. Paul Johansson, President
Elim Bible Institute, Lima, New York

"*The Cry God Answers*, is a heart stirring provocative look at how God intervenes through the miraculous, as our cry rises to Him. Intercessory prayer is the hand that fans revival fires and the means by which God descends from heaven manifesting His glorious restoration. This book will take you beyond the mundane into the fullness of Christ."

Rev. Alvin Miranda, Pastor
Bowling Green, OH

"I have carefully read *The Cry God Answers*, in its entirety and find it to be an excellent work. You have felt God's passion to redeem and restore those souls Satan has tried to destroy. Each chapter opens fresh insight into God's fervent desire to gather the wounded unto Himself. The collective chapters give the effect of looking at a diamond through each of its facets in order to see the whole beauty.

Rev. Norm Whitney
Emerald City Ministries, Seattle, Washington

"Rosemarie Brown's book, *The Cry God Answers*, is a manual for mastery over some of the misunderstood challenges and changes we all encounter. Readers will discover how to turn life's interceptions into liberating intercession, achieving a new level of victory."

Dr. David I. Wyns, Director
Barnabas Ministries, Inc., Rumford, RI

Contents

v

Acknowledgments

My sincere thanks to David, my husband, for his continuous support and encouragement. He willingly took over many domestic chores, freeing my time so that I could write this book.

To Pastor Mary Louise Edlin, heartfelt thanks for challenging me to put this material in writing.

To Pastor David Hernquist, for spiritual leadership and unfailing encouragement to all who attend Van Nest Assembly of God church in the Bronx, special thanks.

To Judy Stefano, special appreciation for her proofreading and excellent recommendations.

To Frank Stefano, grateful recognition for allowing me to share his powerful testimony.

To Patrick Tuminaro, my twin brother, special thanks for his help in proofreading.

Unbounded thanks and appreciation to God for my godly mother, the late Rose Tuminaro, whose walk with God challenged me to follow in her footsteps.

To all my dear friends who have so greatly enriched my life with the treasures of their friendships, I give you thanks.

Foreword

God is full of love and compassion for the human race. He responds especially to the cries of those going through a crisis in their lives. When people cry out to God, He moves to bring release and healing in many forms.

The Cry God Answers describes how God responded to seven individuals in the Word of God as they cried out to Him in their situations. In each case He brought forth victory and blessing that reached beyond their personal lives to affect their nation and the world.

This inspiring book also contains a testimony of someone in our church who received miraculous deliverance from near disaster because he cried out to the Lord in his distress. He is now helping others come out of similar circumstances by the power of God.

Readers will be challenged to take these examples and apply them to their personal lives in order to arrive at a new understanding of the importance and power of intercession. The author, Rosemarie Brown, whose uncle, Rev. Dominick Tuminaro served as pastor here from 1950-1990, is a faithful, submitted, and productive member of this church. Out of a heart that is constantly seeking more of God, Rosemarie is regularly used of the Lord here to touch many lives through her anointed preaching and teaching. I commend this book and the author to you, the reader. May your intimacy with God increase as you meditate on the thoughts contained in this book.

Rev. David H. Hernquist, Pastor
Van Nest Assembly of God
Bronx, New York

Preface

I will stand upon my watch, and set me upon the tower, and will watch to see what he will say unto me, and what I shall answer when I am reproved. And the Lord answered me, and said, Write the vision, and make it plain upon the tables, that he may run that readeth it.

Habukkuk 2:1-2

The contents of this book was originally prepared and presented as a Bible study for the women's ministry of my local church. It is not intended to be a thorough exploration of the topics of restoration and intercessory prayer. Rather, its specific contents came to me in prayer one morning as I sought direction from God on what to speak to the ladies' group.

Ruth, the president of our ladies' fellowship called me on a Thursday evening and asked me to speak at the upcoming ladies' meeting on Monday night. I committed myself to pray and ask God for a fresh word. Early the following morning I began to pray about a message. Immediately, the Holy Spirit spoke these words to my heart, "What is the cry that God answers?"

My mind quickly raced through my own personal struggles with conflict and despair. I recalled times my heart had felt as if it would break from the weight of problems I could not solve. There were times I could not articulate my agony; all I could do was cry out to God and trust Him for deliverance. Scenes flashed before me of occasions when my faith had been tested to its limits—"Did God hear my cry, and would He answer the need of my heart?"

I thought about the day my son was born three months premature, and fighting for his life. After eight years of marriage, I longed to become a mother. I prayed earnestly for this child. Finally, when I did become pregnant, my joy was coupled with several major concerns as I battled physical illness. Fever gripped my body for weeks. As I went into premature labor, my heart sank. I had wondered if my child could survive such an early birth. My mind then returned to the present, and I again focused on the question the Holy Spirit brought before me—"What is the cry that God answers?"

As I meditated on this question, the Holy Spirit took me on a journey. It was as if a curtain had been lifted, and I entered into another realm. In that moment, I saw and heard the cries of seven different individuals from the Old Testament. I watched in amazement. Each one cried out in anguish because of his or her personal crisis. The Holy Spirit tugged at my heart. He showed me how these people prayed and the results God brought through them. I saw that in each case they not only cried out because of their own needs but also the needs of their nation. Each personal crisis was also the crisis of a nation. Through the power of intercession, they not only brought release and victory to their own lives but brought restoration to their nation as well.

In this revelation, my spirit found new release. Praise welled up in my being. I saw the plan of God in a new way. I saw the redemptive value of personal suffering. God had a much broader plan than I had considered. How clearly I saw the truth of God's Word, "They that sow in tears shall reap in joy. He that goeth forth and weepeth, bearing precious seed, shall doubtless come again with rejoicing, bringing his sheaves with him" (Ps. 126:5-6).

In God's presence I lost track of time. It was getting late. I had to get ready for work, but I knew that God had spoken mightily to me. When I returned from work later that day, I made an outline of what I saw and heard in the early morning hours. My sermon was ready for the ladies' meeting!

Monday night at the ladies' meeting, God graciously met us. His glory filled everyone present. As I delivered the word of the Lord that day, there was an awareness within my heart that this word needed to go beyond the borders of this local meeting. The following morning a dear sister from the fellowship called me. Her words still ring in my heart, "Sister Rosemarie, this teaching needs to be put in a book." As she spoke to me, I knew that the Holy Spirit wanted me to write this book.

It is therefore with a spirit of humility and dependence upon the Holy Spirit that I "write the vision, and make it plain upon the tables." I desire to see the Body of Christ strengthened and encouraged as they take their personal sufferings and use them for intercession to bring healing to others who also suffer.

Chapter 1

A New Look at Intercession

Praying always with all prayer and supplication in the Spirit, and watching thereunto with all perseverance and supplication for all saints (Ephesians 6:18).

I exhort therefore, that, first of all, supplications, prayers, intercessions, and giving of thanks, be made for all men (1 Timothy 2:1).

> Their prayers, propelled by the force of their agony, bring healing and restoration to both themselves and those for whom they pray.

Have you ever wondered why Christians suffer? Some people think that when they surrender their lives to Jesus, everything should go easily for them. They believe that the umbrella of God's protection should prevent calamities in their lives—after all, they no longer live under the dominion of sin and their allegiance to Jesus is firm. Yet this is not the case. There is no such thing as immunity from suffering. Suffering surrendered to the Lord actually becomes a mighty tool through which God works out His divine purposes, and Christians must learn how to handle the problem of suffering.

Is there anything that we as Christians can do to expedite a healing process and bring meaning to our suffering? Yes, there is. Discovering wholeness and experiencing healing is often a process that extends over a period of time. For some, complete wholeness is years in the making. For others, there is a quicker release. And for some, there is a continuous striving for the wholeness they desire without ever fully achieving it. The purpose of this study is to offer *one* method by which the Body of Christ can find wholeness and release. We know that God heals and restores in many different ways, but through this study we shall be examining just one of His methods.

No Escape From Trouble

Throughout Scripture the concept of suffering is presented as an inescapable fact of life. Job put it this way, "Yet man is born unto trouble, as the sparks fly upward. ... Man that is born of a woman is of few days, and full of trouble" (Job 5:7; 14:1). Scripture provides us with illustrations of those who suffer because of their own wrongdoing, such as Samson. Samson, a child of promise, chose a wife from the daughters of the Philistines. His disobedience to God eventually caused him great personal suffering.

Scripture also shows us examples of those who suffer because of the wrongdoing of others, persons like Jeremiah. The prophet Jeremiah suffered at the hands of ungodly kings because he boldly declared the judgments of God against them. We also see in Scriptures that there are those who suffer in order that the works of God may be manifested. Concerning the man born blind, Jesus declared, "Neither hath this man sinned, nor his parents: but that the works of God should be made manifest in him" (Jn. 9:3).

As we look at people we know and love, we also see examples of those who suffer because of their own wrongdoing or the wrongdoing of others. I think of little Nina, my former third grade student, and her parents, all victims of AIDS. Nina's parents contracted the HIV virus through their intravenous drug use. As they shared dirty needles, they infected themselves with the deadly virus. By the time Nina was four years old, both of her parents were dead. They were victims of their own wrongdoing. Nina, on the other hand, contracted the HIV virus while still in her mother's womb. She never chose a life of drug addiction. She never used dirty needles. Yet she suffered terribly. AIDS still destroyed her body. She suffered because of the wrongdoing of others.

Our Problems Are Not Unique

Difficulties and struggles in life are not unique to any one individual. Many people suffer in the same way. Although by their description, some would have you believe that their circumstances are worse than others. I am always amazed when I hear remarks such as, "You just would not believe what I am going through," or "This situation is worse than you can ever imagine." These dear folk have not yet realized that everyone suffers in some way. No doubt there are some people who are more vocal about their struggles, while others prefer to keep matters to themselves. Yet regardless of what each situation may be, God's Word sets the record straight:

There hath no temptation taken you but such as is common to man (1 Corinthians 10:13a).

Called to Suffer for Christ

There is a divine call to the Body of Christ to share the sufferings of Christ—a mandate to experience the redemptive value of suffering. What do I mean by the redemptive values of suffering? These are opportunities where God uses suffering for our own good. Here is a brief list of some of the qualities God can develop in us as we submit to the hardships we face.

- Godly character: Our true natures are manifested during times of struggle and difficulty. Here is where the test of Christ-likeness counts. Anyone can be lovely and kind when everything is going well. But it takes God's grace to be sweet under adversity.

- Sensitivity to the needs of others: It is easy to be critical of others and find fault with how they handle their problems—until we have gone through the same trial or difficulty. By our similar experience, we become sensitive to their needs.

- Increase in faith: Nothing builds faith like seeing God at work doing the impossible, especially when His work is in our lives. The more we experience God, the easier it is to believe that He can and will do great things for us.

- Purification and cleansing: Trials and difficulties will manifest the ugliness we harbor within. Under pressure and given the right circumstances, we let it all out. Sometimes we even shock ourselves. We may not have known we were capable of such behavior. But God in His mercy allows us to come face to face with our inner nature in order that He might cleanse and change us.

- Focus on the essential issues of life: Have you ever noticed how some people are always on a fast-paced treadmill and are not going anywhere? They are so wrapped up in their schedules that they have no patience or time for anyone. Suffering can change this. It can bring an individual's focus back to the issues that really matter.

- Identification with Christ: One of the greatest privileges we can have is to become identified with Christ through suffering. In our pain, we see a Savior who willingly endured every imaginable kind of suffering in order that we might be saved. This experience will bring us into a unique oneness with Him.

- Increased capacity for more of God's joy: It is always refreshing to see God's people filled to overflowing with the joy of the Lord. Some of their testimonies reveal an amazing secret. Their joy came as a result of deep sorrow. Instead of developing a root of bitterness, they allowed their suffering to deepen their capacity for more of God's joy.

- Greater appreciation for God's glory: God is longing to teach us many truths by His Spirit. He wants us to partake of His glory. But the pathway to these blessings is often not the one we would choose. However, if we will trust Him in our struggles, He will bring us to heights in God we never knew were possible.

We must understand God's Word regarding suffering, lest we be caught off guard when faced with trouble and our lives become shipwrecked. God's Word to us is so clear.

For unto you it is given in the behalf of Christ, not only to believe on Him, but also to suffer for His sake (Philippians 1:29).

God in His sovereignty has ordained a work of grace through suffering that will not and cannot come any other way. We should not be shocked when we encounter difficulties. God's Word tells us to expect trials and sufferings:

Beloved, think it not strange concerning the fiery trial which is to try you, as though some strange thing happened unto you: but rejoice, inasmuch as ye are partakers of Christ's sufferings; that, when His glory shall be revealed, ye may be glad also with exceeding joy (1 Peter 4:12-13).

As believers, we need to embrace personal suffering. By God's grace we must allow pain and suffering to work for us and not against us. In the midst of our pain, we can find expression and release. We should look at our problems as an opportunity to reach out to help others, much like the way we found our help from the Lord. John Wright Follette in speaking of tribulation had this to say: "It is the use of trouble which releases the deeper springs of our lives and sets aflow the streams of mercy and understanding which a perishing world needs."

Paul, in speaking to the Corinthians, put it this way:

Blessed be God, even the Father of our Lord Jesus Christ, the Father of mercies, and the God of all comfort; who comforteth us in all our tribulation, that we may be able to comfort them which are in any trouble, by the comfort wherewith we ourselves are comforted of God (2 Corinthians 1:3-4).

With suffering comes the temptation to be consumed with personal grief. "Why did this happen to me? I didn't deserve this hardship." As one continues down this path of self-pity, a process of destruction sets in. The purposes of God become blurred as individuals see only their own pain or burden, and they lose their focus on what God wants to accomplish through them. As these persons turn inward, their suffering turns destructive. Disappointment soon gives way to bitterness and disillusionment.

Growing up in my uncle's church, I often heard him say, "Trouble will make you bitter or better." The choice is really ours.

Suffering—A Vehicle for Intercession

The principles of God's Word remain firm in spite of our conflicts and lack of understanding. God's truth is not negated by our ignorance; neither are His purposes diminished when we do not obey His Word. We are called to bear one another's burdens and so fulfill the law of Christ (see Gal. 6:2). God designed the Christian life so that we must pray for each other. As we uphold one another, we bring strength and comfort to the whole Body of Christ. When our prayers reach beyond ourselves, a healing process begins.

God's Word exhorts us to pray for the Body of Christ. "Confess your faults one to another, and pray one for another, that ye may be healed. The effectual fervent prayer of a righteous man availeth much" (Jas. 5:16). Our failure in this mission to pray for others will not change God's plan. God will not change His standard because we miss His purposes. However, our failure to pray for others leaves a weakness, or a lack, within the Church.

God's purposes remain the same today. He wants to bring life and hope to those who suffer. He wants to bring healing and restoration to the Body of Christ. God is looking for those individuals who, in their pain, will offer themselves as intercessors for others. *Personal pain and suffering are the vehicle through which believers become able to cry out against that which plagues them and to cry out on behalf of others for whom they intercede. Their cries become their mission. Their prayers, propelled by the force of their agony, bring healing and restoration to both themselves and those for whom they pray.*

What Is Intercession?

Intercession can be defined as the act of petitioning God, or praying on behalf of another person or group. The primary Greek noun for intercession is *enteuxis* (Strong's #1783), which means "a petition."[1] It is used as a technical term for approaching a king. In First Timothy 2:1, Christians are urged to intercede for all people, "seeking the presence and hearing of God on behalf of others." The Greek verb for intercession is *entungchano* (Strong's #1973), which means to "fall in with, meet with in order to converse." It also means "to make petition especially to make intercession, plead with a person, either for or against others." An example of its usage can be found in Romans 8:27 where we are told that the Holy Spirit pleads on behalf of the individual Christian.

History has been marked by great men and women of God who gave themselves as intercessors in the work God called them to do. One such example was Rees Howells. In his excellent biography *Rees Howells Intercessor*, Norman Grubb lists three things that will be seen in the prayer of an intercessor that are not necessarily found in ordinary prayer: identification, agony, and authority. Grubb goes on to describe identification as the process by which the intercessor "pleads effectively because he gives his life for those he pleads for; he is their genuine representative; he has submerged his

---

1. James Strong, *The Exhaustive Concordance of the Bible* (Peabody, MA: Hendrickson Publishers, n.d.).

self-interest in their needs and sufferings, and as far as possible has literally taken their place."[2] Scripture describes the agony of this ministry of intercession as the work of the Holy Spirit where the "Spirit... maketh intercession for us with groanings which cannot be uttered" (Rom. 8:26b). Individuals become intercessors by reason of the Intercessor within them.

"But intercession is more than the Spirit sharing His groanings with us and living His life of sacrifice for the world through us. It is the Spirit gaining His ends of abundant grace. If the intercessor knows identification and agony, he also knows authority. It is the law of the corn of wheat and the harvest: 'If it die, it bringeth forth much fruit.' Because the intercessor so identifies with the sufferer, he gains 'a prevailing place with God. He moves God.' "[3]

A Womb for God

Throughout Scripture, we are given repeated examples of individuals whose personal cries brought corporate results. The effect of their prayers touched the lives of others within the area of

---

2. Norman Grubb, *Rees Howells Intercessor* (Fort Washington: Christian Literature Crusade, 1994), p. 82. Used by permission.
3. Grubb, *Rees Howells*, p. 84.

---

their influence. We will examine seven such individuals—Moses, Jonah, Nehemiah, Esther, Hannah, David, and Joseph. These are people whose cries in their crises not only released themselves, but through their intercession brought deliverance on a much larger scale. The prayers and actions of these persons brought national results. These people were impregnated with the purposes of God, which carried them to a place of divine fulfillment and destiny. By way of their abandonment to God, these individuals gave themselves as a womb to carry the burden of the Lord to a place of vibrant life. Their testimonies provide us an example to also "travail in birth again until Christ be formed" in the lives of those to whom we minister (see Gal. 4:19).

Let us release the power of God through prayer, and not limit it because of our ignorance. Let us realize that effectual, fervent prayer "availeth much"—far beyond the borders of our needs, burdens, and situations. Let us each offer ourselves as a womb for God's purpose; let us be people in whom He can entrust His burden and His purposes. Let us determine that we will not miscarry or abort that which He places within us. But we will be faithful to bring to birth new life as His Spirit prays through us.

Missed Opportunities

We have each missed opportunities where God could have used us as intercessors to reach beyond our needs, but our vision was shortsighted. We only saw our own problems, and we only prayed for our own release. I am reminded of dear precious friends, men and women of God, who earnestly sought God for answers. In times of crisis they found personal victories as they prayed. But their prayers were limited to only their concerns. I can still see the brokenness of Betty's face as she came to talk with me. She found out that her husband was involved with another woman. Unable to sleep and unable to eat, she began to lose weight rapidly. She needed a miracle in her home. We agreed to meet together for prayer on a regular basis. God was faithful. As we prayed, changes began to take place. Her husband and her marriage were sovereignly put back together. At that time neither of us thought to use this opportunity to pray for other couples who struggled with the same problem. We missed an opportunity to go beyond her immediate need and see a much larger picture—couples we both knew who were also devastated by unfaithfulness.

The same energy we use to pray for our personal needs can also be channeled for the needs of others. We need to ask ourselves, "How many others are going through the same thing I am going through right now? Could I not expand the scope of my horizon by praying for others with my same problem? Could I not let the intensity of my cry also avail on behalf of others?" It is this type of prayer that will change our world.

People Find Healings as They Pray for Others

Prior to the preparation of this manuscript, I conducted several conferences based upon this material. In each case, the effect was amazing. Without exception, person after person found a way in which they could put their personal pain into a context of meaning and purpose.

For the first time, many people saw their suffering from a redemptive view—one in which they could find healing for themselves and for others. No longer did they see themselves as victims, suffering the injustices of a cruel world. God had not abandoned them in their pain. Rather they saw themselves as part of the plan of God. God was motivating them to a place of action and a place of healing. Tears of relief streamed down the faces of praying believers. New understanding replaced old thoughts. For each one, the healing journey had begun.

A rather amazing event took place in one women's conference. Many of the women immediately latched on to the concept that God was looking for a womb in which He could bring His purposes to birth. In response to the Spirit's call, they swiftly changed gears in their prayer. Their prayers took on a new sound. No longer did they cry out for their own needs, even though their needs were great. Cries of intercession filled the room.

These women were now praying for others who shared their struggles. It wasn't long before I saw the fruit of their labor. One by one, women began to exclaim, "I'm healed, I'm healed." Faces were radiant with victory.

Later, as I talked with these women, I realized that even though their circumstances may have remained the same, they were set free. Change had taken place on the inside, where it really counted. There was new strength and determination to tackle old problems. None of us who left the conference that day had any doubt that great healings had taken place.

Thank God that the ministry of intercession and the glory of restoration continue mightily, as men and women give themselves to prayer. Only eternity will reveal the untold, powerful victories wrought by God because people prayed—the victories and testimonies of those who "cried unto the Lord in their trouble, and He delivered them out of their distresses" (Ps. 107:6). It is glorious to see God bring deliverance to an individual's life. But it is exceedingly glorious to see God bring the same deliverance to others because of the personal victories of individuals.

Up Close and Personal—A Modern Day Cry

Frank's Story

Frank and his wife Judy are the leaders of New Creations in Christ, a dynamic ministry in the local church of Van Nest Assembly of God, Bronx, New York. This ministry is an outreach and support system for those overcoming life-controlling problems, including drug and alcohol addictions.

In their weekly meetings, Frank and Judy touch dozens of lives as they give themselves to God and His people. Scores of people have been saved, delivered, and restored through this powerful ministry. But it wasn't always this way. Frank had a very different life prior to coming to Christ. He had been a victim of sin's captivity. Trapped by homosexuality, drugs, and alcohol, Frank lived as an emotional wreck in the streets of New York City. With no self-respect and no prospects for the future, Frank often ran the streets as he wasted the gift of life.

How did Frank fall prey to so many problems? It was because his life was as the city of Jerusalem in the days of Nehemiah; his walls of support and protection were broken down. Gates through which the Lord could have found passage had been burned with fire (see Neh. 1:3). When Frank's life was left vulnerable and exposed, the enemy made his entrance. Frank's father left home, leaving his young mother burdened with the care of the young children. She was filled with hurt, anger, bitterness, and fear. Because she herself was so needy, she was unable to recognize or meet Frank's growing needs.

Sexually molested at the age of eight years old by older teenage boys, Frank was left with a lasting sense of guilt and mistrust. Walls continued to crumble about him. Alcohol and drugs became substitutes for comfort and security. Frank's sexual identity was further destroyed as he also struggled with a physical defect in his male organs. Years later corrective surgery would take place but by then the emotional damage was done. Feelings of inadequacy continued to mount in his life, which opened the door to deviant sexual behaviors. Frank's struggle with a learning disability added to his grief. Every academic task represented a mountain of impossibility. Frank told himself repeatedly that he couldn't learn and that he was a failure. His thoughts were dominated by negative thinking. Life had no meaning. He had lost all self-respect and wanted to die.

In despair, Frank cried out to God. He knew he needed a miracle. Sometimes as Frank watched television, he saw evangelists preach about a loving God who could change people's lives. His heart was gripped. He wondered, "Could this be for me?" As he watched the television evangelists, he often placed his hands on the television screen as they prayed, hoping that their prayers would also help him. Although he cursed and hated God, he knew deep inside that only God could help him.

In the providence of God, Frank went to a methadone clinic where he was linked up with a

Christian counselor who shared the Word of God with him. Slowly, very slowly, Frank's broken walls were rebuilt. Support systems came together. With encouragement from his Christian counselor, Frank attended Alcoholics Anonymous, Narcotics Anonymous, and church meetings. One by one, God brought powerful friends into Frank's life. One special friend, Steve Dellacese, became his mentor. Steve understood Frank's pain. He himself had overcome a life of drug addition. The victory in Steve's life was encouraging. Steve shared his heart and life with Frank and placed a great deposit of God and a love for the Scriptures within him. Something wonderful became ignited within Frank's life.

God not only heard Frank's cry for help but gloriously saved him and filled him with the Holy Spirit. It has been over 12 years since Frank has used either drugs or alcohol. For the past 11 years Frank has been part of the Van Nest Assembly of God church, and God's grace continues to work mightily in his life.

Everything about Frank's life has changed! Frank has become a man of prayer. He realized that his cry to God was also the cry of multitudes who are suffering the ravages of sin's destructive power. He began to seek God on behalf of those who suffered as he once did. In time, Frank's burden and intercession for the victims of life-controlling problems gripped his heart and life to the point that he could no longer sit in the background. It compelled him to a place of active ministry. He began by reaching one person at a time. Frank often pours his life into other people as he ministers to them. He knows what it means to "sit where they sit." Now Frank repairs broken walls in the lives of those who suffer as he once did. With the love of God and the power of the Holy Spirit working through him, Frank is able to provide support and comfort to those who have no hope. He proclaims the glorious message of salvation with confidence and assurance.

Along with the ministry and support group of New Creations in Christ, Frank also coordinates a ministry to the homeless that includes street evangelism. As a team leader, Frank and other workers from Van Nest distribute gospel literature, food, clothing, and toiletries as they share their testimonies with the destitute. Frank also visits those who are sick with the AIDS virus both in the hospital and in their homes.

Other doors of ministry have also opened for Frank. God has blessed him with a godly helpmate, and on Friday evenings, he and his wife Judy work with children at the Van Nest Assembly of God church. There he shares with the children the love and joy God has given him. In fact, Frank radiates the joy of the Lord. God not only delivered him inwardly, but outwardly as well. With nothing to fear and nothing to hide, Frank has become transparent for all to see the glory of God in his life. Frank has become a responsible, honest, and willing servant of the Lord. He has found the love, joy, and peace for which he always searched. His world is now beautiful!

The grace of God in Frank's life has also been extended to his family. Relationships have been restored. Discord has been replaced with harmony and friendship. Today, Frank is able to provide love and support to his mother, brother, and two sisters. He and his father share a close relationship—something Frank always desired but could not achieve on his own.

All this has been accomplished in spite of his learning disability. Once Frank felt inferior and inadequate, but now Frank is a leader. He recognizes that the Spirit of the Lord is within him. And that makes all the difference. Frank and Judy are devoted to sharing God's glorious message of restoration, and their lives continually demonstrate to a hurting city *The Cry God Answers*!

Chapter 2

Moses: A Cry for Freedom

*And Pharaoh charged all his people, saying, Every son that is born ye shall cast into the river, and every daughter ye shall save alive. And there went a man of the house of Levi, and took to wife a daughter of Levi. And the woman conceived, and bare a son: and when she saw him that he was a goodly child, she hid him three months. And when she could not longer hide him, she took for him an ark of bulrushes, and daubed it with slime and with pitch, and put the child therein; and she laid it in the flags by the river's brink. And his sister stood afar off, to wit what would be done to him. And the daughter of Pharaoh came down to wash herself at the river; and her maidens walked along by the river's side; and when she saw the ark among the flags, she sent her maid to fetch it. And when she had opened it, she saw the child: **and, behold,*** *the babe wept. And she had compassion on him, and said, This is one of the Hebrews' children* (Exodus 1:22–2:6).

> Moses, by reason of his circumstance, became a type of a nation he would one day lead.

Freedom is a word many of us take for granted. The Declaration of Independence upon which our country was founded establishes that we are each entitled to certain rights—the right to life, liberty, and the pursuit of happiness. Sometimes we forget that our forefathers fought vigorously, sacrificing their lives for the freedom we now enjoy. Yet for many, freedom is still an elusive dream. The cry within the human breast rings loud and clear, "Let my people go." It is a cry that is common to all people everywhere. It is a cry placed within the heart of man by God Himself.

In the passage from Exodus above, we are told of the cry of baby Moses. The scene takes place in Egypt during a time of great political turmoil. The children of Israel lived in bondage and repression in a strange land. Without citizenship and without rights, they endured the hardships of slaves. Because their very existence was a threat to Pharaoh, he made them outcasts, victims of racial prejudice. It was obvious that the blessings of God were upon them:

And the children of Israel were fruitful, and increased abundantly, and multiplied, and waxed exceeding mighty; and the land was filled with them (Exodus 1:7).

Their prosperity was the fulfillment of God's promise to Abraham, to whom God had promised:

And I will make of thee a great nation, and I will bless thee, and make thy name great; and thou shalt be a blessing: ... And I will make thy seed as the dust of the earth: so that if a man can number the dust of the earth, then shall thy seed also be numbered (Genesis 12:2; 13:16).

Settling for Less Than God's Best

Years before the birth of Moses, Jacob's sons had come to Egypt seeking relief from famine. They were welcomed with open arms by their brother Joseph and the pharaoh he served. It was never their intention to make Egypt a place of permanent residence. Rather, they became comfortable in a land that had opened its doors to them in their time of need. But God's plan for Israel was still the promised land—the land of Canaan. He wanted His people to enjoy the privilege of relationship without the repression of bondage. In His mercy, He allowed circumstances of adversity in order to bring about change. For as long as Israel was comfortable with less than God's best, no movement would be made to go to the land of promise.

God Uses Adversity to Change Us

God's use of adversity in the life and story of Moses is not unique. This pattern is repeated throughout Scripture. Recall for a moment the powerful story of Ruth and Naomi. Elimelech, his wife Naomi, and their two sons lived in the land of Bethlehem-Judah during the time of great famine. Their temporary "sojourn" to the land of Moab in search of food extended well beyond the drought of their homeland. Ten long and difficult years passed—years of heartache and death. Elimelech died in that pagan land of Moab, along with his two sons, Mahlon and Chilion. Both sons left behind Moabite wives, women whom they had married during their ten-year stay in a foreign land. Propelled by these catastrophic events Naomi returned to Bethlehem. God had allowed the push and pull of circumstances to drive Naomi to the place where His divine purposes could be fulfilled through her.

It's sad, but at times we also are guilty of the same thing. We settle for less than God's best. Often God has to shake us in order to get us to where we belong in Him. In His great love, He will allow adversity to stimulate and motivate us to move on in Him. As we cry out to Him, He will reveal a plan that goes beyond our present circumstances. Then with new vision we will move into the place of His choosing—a place of freedom and blessing.

God Works Behind the Scenes to Bring About His Purposes

When the Hebrews first moved to Egypt it was the result of famine in their land. God had provided for them by placing Joseph into a position of power and authority in the government of that country. God never intended their stay to be a permanent one, and He blessed them in that land. They became comfortable and settled in. They lost their desire to return to the land of promise that God had promised to their forefathers. So in time, a new king came to reign over Egypt. He was not sympathetic to the Hebrews, nor to the provisions made by his ancestor who had ruled Egypt during the days of Joseph. He saw the children of Israel as "more and mightier" than his own Egyptians. His fear caused him to make them slaves. He hoped that affliction would bring the downfall of the Hebrew people.

But the more [the Egyptians] *afflicted them, the more they multiplied and grew. And they were grieved because of the children of Israel* (Exodus 1:12).

Frustrated by the failure of his first plan, Pharaoh's new plan instructed the midwives to kill all the baby boys born to the Hebrew women and throw them into the river. Born in the midst of this conflict to godly parents who were not afraid of the king's commandment, Moses was hidden at home for three months. When he could no longer be hidden, his mother Jochebed made him "an ark of bulrushes, and daubed it with slime and with pitch," placed him inside, and put the ark by the river's bank (Ex. 2:3). Although it may have seemed that Moses was abandoned by the mother who so dearly loved and cherished him, it was really her abandonment to God that allowed her to release this baby to the care of his heavenly Father.

One can only attempt to imagine the thoughts that passed through the minds of Jochebed and the baby's sister Miriam as they looked on from a distance. Did they struggle with doubt or fear, or did they stand firm in their hour of testing? Perhaps they felt the way we would have felt under these circumstances. In my heart I can almost hear Jochebed cry out, "Lord, I believe. Help my unbelief. I have always trusted You. Help me to trust You now, even when I don't see an answer. Please make a way for my baby to live. I will dedicate him wholly unto You." And Miriam was yet in her youth, not yet mature in the ways of God. Did she feel as if her heart would break from not knowing what would become of her baby brother? It was by faith that Jochebed placed her confidence in God.

The Providence of God

Through the providence of God, baby Moses was discovered by Pharaoh's daughter, who happened to be bathing nearby. From his small ark on the riverbank, Moses let out a cry. His cry reached right into the heart of Pharaoh's daughter and made provision for his rescue and salvation. What irony! Pharaoh sought to destroy the Hebrew boys; Pharaoh's daughter made provision for their rescue. Contained within the cry of Moses was the cry of an entire nation. Moses, by reason of his circumstance, became a type of a nation he would one day lead.

The Cry of Moses Represents the Cry of a Nation

A Cry for Salvation

The symbolism is so clear. In the cry of Moses we can hear a cry for salvation. The baby Moses faced certain death unless he was plucked from the waters of the Nile. Unless Israel was saved from the dominion of Pharaoh, they faced the threat of planned extinction.

A Cry Against Racial Prejudice

In the cry of Moses we hear a cry to be delivered from racial prejudice and wicked political devices. Pharaoh had charged that all Hebrew boys were to be killed. Moses was about to become a casualty of the most severe form of racism. The children of Israel were suffering extreme repression and bondage. They understood the stigma of racial prejudice, and they cried out to God for their deliverance. They knew that the change they needed could not be negotiated through political systems. It had to be brought about through divine intervention.

A Cry for Nurturing

How long was Moses in that woven basket? How long did he cry for his mother and find no response? In the cry of Moses we hear a cry to be nurtured. He longed to be embraced and comforted by his mother's tender touch. It wasn't enough for him to be rescued from the water; someone had to love him, feed him, and care for him—moment by moment and day by day.

Yet in one moment, what seemed so hopeless and so impossible was suddenly changed by the power of God. The Holy Spirit quickened Miriam as she watched her brother from a distance. Inspired by the princess' compassion for her baby brother, Miriam quickly seized the opportunity to ask Pharaoh's daughter, "Shall I go and call to thee a nurse of the Hebrew women, that she may nurse the child for thee?" (Ex. 2:7b) At her tender young age, Miriam witnessed for herself the demonstration of God's miraculous power. What joy must have filled their hearts as Miriam returned with the child's own mother and presented her to be the Hebrew nurse to care for this baby!

Israel needed to be nurtured and cared for. A stranger would not do. Only one of their own could feel the compassion needed to tenderly lead them. God found that kinship in Moses. Here was a man who would so identify with Israel, he would one day petition God to have his own name removed from the book of life rather than see his people lost.

A Corporate Cry of the Hebrew Children

In the cry of Moses we hear the cry of his Hebrew brethren, a cry that would one day lead him to be a great intercessor and a great deliverer.

And it came to pass in the process of time, that the king of Egypt died: and the children of Israel sighed by reason of the bondage, and they cried, and their cry came up unto God by reason of the bondage. And God heard their groaning, and God remembered His covenant with Abraham, with Isaac, and with Jacob (Exodus 2:23-24).

And the Lord said, I have surely seen the affliction of My people which are in Egypt, and have heard their cry by reason of their taskmasters; for I know their sorrows; and I am come down to deliver them out of the hand of the Egyptians... (Exodus 3:7-8).

By the plan of God, Moses tasted on a personal level the very heartache he would cry against on a national level. Did he not cry for salvation? Did he not cry against racial prejudice and political wickedness? Did he not cry for nurture and for care?

It was the extremity and heartache of his personal experience that enabled him to be sensitive to the very same cries of a nation. When Israel cried "by reason of the bondage," God knew He could find in Moses an empathetic servant. The agony of his personal experience became the backdrop of his future ministry.

God's call to Moses and his subsequent preparation was because God:

1. Heard the people groaning (Ex. 2:24);
2. Saw their affliction (Ex. 3:7);
3. Knew their sorrows (Ex. 3:7);
4. Was mindful of His covenant (Ex. 2:24).

The life of Moses clearly illustrates the releasing of a personal cry and the demonstration of a corporate response. As a stranger in a strange land, Moses empathized with the plight of his Hebrew brothers who were also strangers in a strange land—in need of a deliverer who would lead them to the land of promise.

Moses still had to learn the ways of God. Like many of us, he struggled with God's timing. His initial attempt to deliver God's people failed because he allowed the dictates of his flesh to control his actions rather than the prompting of the Holy Spirit. Therefore, God had to take Moses into the desert to strip him of all self-sufficiency. After 40 years in the backside of a desert, God revealed Himself to Moses. Conscious of the fact that he was now a "nobody," Moses objected to his call. To each of his objections God had a reply:

1. Objection—Lack of qualification—"Who am I?" (Ex. 3:11),
God's Response—"Certainly I will be with thee" (Ex. 3:12).

2. Objection—Lack of subject matter—"What shall I say unto them?" (Ex. 3:13),
God's Response—"I AM hath sent me" (Ex. 3:14).

3. Objection—Lack of credentials—"They will say, 'The Lord hath not appeared unto thee' " (Ex. 4:1),
God's Response—"What is that in thine hand?" (Ex. 4:2).

4. Objection—Lack of eloquence—"I am not eloquent...but I am slow of speech, and of a slow tongue" (Ex. 4:10),
God's Response—"I will be with thy mouth" (Ex. 4:12).

A Life Marked by Intercession

The providential path of Moses' own experience prepared and qualified him for leadership. His intercession on behalf of Israel was a mark of his greatness. This intercessory cry was often repeated throughout his ministry. When Israel sinned by worshipping the golden calf, it was the cry of Moses that spared their lives from the judgment of God. On another occasion God wanted to destroy the children of Israel because of their unbelief and their adherence to the negative report of the spies; again the intercession of Moses worked to bring them pardon from the Lord.

The intercession was not always alone. On one occasion the burden of intercession required the assistance of Aaron and Hur to keep his hands uplifted until the sun set as the children of Israel battled the Amalekites. Let us also learn the valuable lesson of assistance from others in the work of intercession. If Moses needed help in battling the forces of the enemy, we too will have occasions when we cannot prevail by ourselves. This is not a sign of weakness. Rather, it is an indication of the fierceness of the battle. God wants us to join with those who will intercede with us. Together we will see the work of satan defeated. Only as the Church marches forward on her knees will the forces of satan be pushed back.

Pain Brings Purpose

How different the scriptural account would have been if Moses had allowed bitterness to control his thoughts. If Moses had focused on his own pain and the unfortunate circumstances of his life, he never would have achieved the position of a leader. Moses became a mighty instrument for God by channeling the disappointments of his past into a life message of intercession. *No longer did his own pain become a snare. Rather, Moses brought significance and meaning to his pain as he cried out to God for others who suffered as he once did.* By so doing, he brought restoration and healing not only to his own life, but to a nation. Because Moses became an intercessor, a people was preserved, a nation was restored, and the plan of satan was defeated.

How does this relate to us today? The Old Testament accounts of great men and women of God are more than a recording of historical events. They are written for our benefit, that we might learn from the experiences of these people of faith. Their failures warn us to avoid the same mistakes. Their victories declare what God can and will do in our lives. Shall we not determine to let God have His way in us? There are no wasted experiences in Him. Everything submitted to the Lord can work for our eternal good. By faith, release to God every area of hurt and misunderstanding. Let Him bring purpose and meaning to each area.

Now these things were our examples, to the intent we should not lust after evil things, as they also lusted. ... Now all these things happened unto them for ensamples: and they are written for our admonition, upon whom the ends of the world are come (1 Corinthians 10:6,11).

Heavenly Father, we thank You that You have heard the cry of our hearts. In Your great love, You purchased our freedom with the precious blood of the Lord Jesus. No longer do we want to complain as those who have no hope. Rather, we want to see Your purposes in all the struggles we go through. We want to be instruments of Your glory and grace. Help us as we give ourselves as intercessors on behalf of those who suffer as we do. Grant unto us a true spirit of supplication. Teach us how to pray. Give us a vision of Your greatness. We pray for a fresh infilling of Your Holy Spirit and pray that Your power be greatly manifested through us, bringing healing and deliverance to those in need. Amen.

Personal Reflections

As we study the life of Moses and the lifestyle of the Hebrews prior to their exodus, we can easily imagine the array of feelings they must have had. They are feelings many of us can recognize in our life or the lives of people we know.

- Rejection
- Abandonment
- Victimization through racism
- Isolation
- Vulnerability
- Desperation
- Hopelessness

Take Action—Record Your Personal Inventory

1. As you review the above list, which feelings do you share with Moses and the children of Israel?

2. What heartaches have you experienced that caused these feelings to develop? List the causes responsible for your heartache and cry to God.

3. How would you describe your cry?

4. What percentage of your life does your cry dominate?

Take Action—Look for Personal Healing

1. In what ways did hardship contribute to Moses' effective leadership of his nation?

2. In what ways could your hardships contribute to your future success?

3. Rather than be consumed with personal grief, what practical steps can you take to alleviate your pain?

4. Explain one positive way you can redirect your energies.

Take Action—Become an Intercessor

1. Name other people you know who have experienced heartaches similar to your own.

2. Describe the last time you seriously prayed about the struggles you and these other people share.

3. Realize you are not alone in your problems. Consider ways the releasing of your emotions in prayer can bring healing to you and others who share the same pain.

4. Explain how your once negative feelings can give positive energy to your prayers.

Take Action—Reach Out and Help Others

1. In what ways could your triumph become a life-giving message to others who suffer?

2. How can you share your victory with others?

Chapter 3

Jonah: A Cry for Repentance

Then Jonah prayed unto the Lord his God out of the fish's belly, and said, I cried by reason of mine affliction unto the Lord, and He heard me; out of the belly of hell cried I, and Thou heardest my voice. ... Then I said, I am cast out of Thy sight; yet I will look again toward Thy holy temple. ...yet hast Thou brought up my life from corruption, O Lord my God. When my soul fainted within me I remembered the Lord: and my prayer came in unto Thee, into Thine holy temple. They that observe lying vanities forsake their own mercy. But I will sacrifice unto Thee with the voice of thanksgiving; I will pay that that I have vowed. Salvation is of the Lord (Jonah 2:1-2,4,6-9).

The reach of God extends beyond the borders of our disobedience and failure.

Desperation leads many people to do what they normally would not do. In fact, it can even cause men and women to cry out to God in repentance. If we were able to examine the motives of everyone who committed their lives to the Lord Jesus, how surprised would we really be? No doubt many people come to the Lord because of the extremity of their circumstances. The consequences of their sin have driven them to a place where God is their only hope. The Book of Jonah provides us with an excellent example of the type of desperation that leads to repentance.

The passage quoted earlier relates Jonah's cry of distress as he fought for his life. Jonah's disobedience brought him to this place of extremity. Little is known about the life and background of Jonah except that he was a prophet from Gath-hepher. The Book of Jonah provides the historical account of Jonah's personal experience, his prophetic call to Nineveh, his rebellion against the call of God, and his subsequent obedience.

The Disobedience

Our first introduction to Jonah is to that of a disobedient prophet. God clearly commissioned him to go to Nineveh, the capital city of Assyria, and cry against their wickedness. Instead of obeying God and delivering God's message, he chose to flee in the opposite direction to the city of Tarshish. Jonah thought he could choose his own way. Consequently, he allowed his own logic and feelings to determine his course of action. Without stopping to pray about his decision or receive clearance from God regarding his plans, he fled from the presence of God.

His disobedience to God and willful, selfish behavior lay in his knowledge that God would extend mercy to the Ninevites if they repented. Assyria, the enemy of Israel, was notorious for its evil empire and its heartless acts of cruelty. Jonah did not want God to show mercy to the enemies of his people. His hatred for the wicked Assyrians caused him to look for vengeance, not salvation. So Jonah put his patriotism above the will of God. Jonah justified his course of action in his mind. Nineveh did not deserve the mercy of God. Therefore, he was not going to do anything in his ministry that might assist them in obtaining God's favor.

Jonah refused to obey God for other personal reasons as well. He was concerned about his reputation, particularly his credibility as a prophet. Just suppose Nineveh repented, how would the "religious experts" of his day view the authenticity of his message? He was called to pronounce judgment, "*yet forty days, and Nineveh shall be overthrown*," not preach a salvation message (Jon. 3:4). Jonah had no intention of concluding his sermon with an altar call. He was not interested in seeing anyone repent or find salvation. He wanted to see the wrath of God fall upon these wicked people. Wouldn't the sparing of Nineveh permit people to question Jonah's prophetic pronouncement? Jonah thought so. Therefore, he guarded his pride and disobeyed God.

Before we become too critical of Jonah and his disobedience, let us realize that it is one thing to receive a call from God and quite another to follow through with that call. When God speaks to us, He is not looking for our reasons why we should or should not do what He asks. Rather, He is looking for servants who trust Him completely and will follow Him without reservation.

The Affliction

Jonah's willful disobedience brought him to a place of extreme calamity. Jonah thought he could run from God, but God knew where to find him. God knew how to get his attention and the attention of all those with him. He sent a fierce storm that overtook the ship Jonah was on. It was about to sink. Everyone aboard was in peril, and Jonah was responsible. What he had done in secret was now openly manifested. With nowhere to hide, Jonah made full confession to the mariners. It was clear to Jonah that the storm they encountered was the result of his sin. In order to preserve the lives of the innocent mariners, Jonah asked that he be thrown overboard. Immediately the storm stopped.

In that moment Jonah became an outcast. He also became a type of Nineveh, the outcast city that was to be miraculously preserved through the ministry of one who had also rejected it. As he was cast out of that ship, all Jonah's hopes for the future vanished. He was forced to face the dismal failure of his own ways. Jonah was no longer interested in his own pursuits. His agenda came to a dramatic end. There was nowhere to turn. Finally, Jonah was at a place where God could touch him. God had a plan. He would take this awful crisis and bring meaning to Jonah's personal pain.

The Cry

Entombed within the belly of a fish, Jonah confronted his hopeless situation. His desperation caused him to cry out to God. In his plight, Jonah's cry represented the cry of all Nineveh. Like Jonah, this city certainly seemed doomed. Had not God commanded him to preach judgment?

Arise, go to Nineveh, that great city, and cry against it; for their wickedness is come up before Me (Jonah 1:2).

Jonah's message would be brief and to the point:

Yet forty days, and Nineveh shall be overthrown (Jonah 3:4b).

How could God not judge a people who appeared to be beyond redemption? Keenly aware of His divine displeasure, Jonah dared to look to God in the severity of his own circumstances because he knew something of the mercy of God. Hoping against hope, Jonah cried out to God. This personal cry for mercy contained the corporate cry of a people in great need of God's mercy. Let us note some important qualities in Jonah's prayer.

- He resorted to God in the midst of hopeless circumstances (Jon. 2:1,7).

- His earnest and loud cry was caused by severe affliction (Jon. 2:2).

- He acknowledged his plight was a result of his own disobedience (Jon. 2:3).

- He was aware of God's displeasure, yet he dared to approach God and look to Him again (Jon. 2:4).

- The hopelessness of his situation did not prevent God from bringing deliverance (Jon. 2:5-6).

- He recognized his own ways as deceiving and worthless (Jon. 2:8).

- He arrived at a place of rededication and submission (Jon. 2:9).

- He understood the importance of thanksgiving (Jon. 2:9).

- He knew salvation is only from God (Jon. 2:9).

- When he submitted himself to God's purposes, he received a response from God (Jon. 2:10).

Even from Jonah's point of view, his prayer and the ensuing results were totally remarkable. Through his words, the key principles of prayer are clearly illustrated:

- The *Purpose* of Prayer—"I cried by reason of mine affliction" (Jon. 2:2);

- The *Place* of Prayer—"Out of the belly of hell" (Jon. 2:2);

- The *Provision* of Prayer—"He heard me" (Jon. 2:2);

- The *Perception* in Prayer—"I am cast out of Thy sight" (Jon. 2:4);

- The *Power* of Prayer—"My prayer came in unto Thee, into Thine holy temple" (Jon. 2:7).

The Deliverance

The hopelessness of Jonah's predicament did not prevent God from bringing deliverance. It took the extremity of Jonah's circumstance for him to recognize the futility of his own pursuits apart from the will of God. With this recognition came submission to the purposes of God. Like Moses, Jonah had to be completely stripped of self. God now had Jonah in the place where He could again use him for His glory. Once Jonah responded to the will of

God, God commanded the fish to deliver Jonah on dry land.

So it was that Nineveh, in the extremity of its circumstance, was also brought to a place of humility, repentance, and submission to God. The people of Nineveh received the message of judgment delivered by Jonah and believed God. As Jonah spoke those life-changing words, he also communicated their reality. The people knew their doom was at hand. In response to God's pronouncement, they "proclaimed a fast and put on sackcloth, from the greatest of them even to the least of them" (Jon. 3:5). Even the king laid aside his kingly robe and arose from his throne. He too needed to cry out to God for mercy. So seriously did they take God's message of judgment that they included their animals in this fast. Their fast was symbolic of their penitence, humility, urgency, and petition before God. The sincerity of their repentance was evident everywhere. A city once known for its evil actions changed overnight. In response to that repentance God delivered Nineveh despite the hopeless nature of the circumstances.

So the people of Nineveh believed God, and proclaimed a fast, and put on sackcloth, from the greatest of them even to the least of them. ... But let man and beast be covered with sackcloth, and cry mightily unto God: yea, let them turn every one from his evil way, and from the violence that is in their hands. Who can tell if God will turn and repent, and turn away from His fierce anger, that we perish not? And God saw their works, that they turned from their evil way; and God repented of the evil, that He had said that He would do unto them; and He did it not (Jonah 3:5,8-10).

At no time in telling this story did Jonah try to make himself look good. He suffered from a bad attitude that greatly affected his ministry and almost cost him everything, including his life. Even when Nineveh repented and God spared them from the judgment against them, Jonah did not rejoice. In fact, he complained bitterly. He still failed to understand the greatness of God's mercy. Even though Jonah, like Nineveh, had experienced mercy when he deserved judgment, he continued to struggle. God's mercy far surpassed Jonah's ability to reason it out.

It is important to remember that in narrating his own experience, Jonah intentionally includes some information, while excluding other details. Clearly, his message teaches us the all-inclusiveness of the mercy of God. The national prejudice of the Hebrew people against other peoples is also openly demonstrated. Through relating this one experience of personal failure, Jonah obviously intended to teach others the lesson he had learned. However, Jonah's exclusion of personal virtues or his prophetic ministry emphasizes the fact that God did what Jonah could not do.

With great humility, Jonah refused to take credit for the work of God. Although Jonah had total victory in the end, he allowed it to be camouflaged in order that the message of God's goodness would stand out in contrast to his own prejudice and disobedience. Let us not forget that God called Jonah *His* servant and prophet (see 2 Kings 14:25). Certainly Jonah's life and ministry included periods of intercession and victories that are not recorded in Scripture.

What a message his example provides to all of us who feel that we may have transgressed beyond the point of no return—that we have sinned beyond the point of redemption. Through Jonah God clearly demonstrates His mercy, even when all natural circumstances point to total loss. The reach of God can always extend past the borders of our personal disobedience and failure.

The Book of Jonah also exhibits a marvelous cry from God's own heart. Four times within this narrative we have the expression "the Lord prepared." In this story God's cry, the desires of His heart for His people, is demonstrated through His preparation of four things—the great fish, the gourd, the worm, and the vehement east wind.

The Great Fish

Now the Lord had prepared a great fish to swallow up Jonah. And Jonah was in the belly of the fish three days and three nights (Jonah 1:17).

The fish served as a chapel for contrition. With no place to go and no way to escape, the fish God prepared gave Jonah time to think, pray, and repent. As Jonah was held captive against his own will, he was brought to a place where his will entered into submission to the will of God. Repentance is always paramount to God. Perhaps we can each recall times when God allowed extreme measures to come our way in order that His purposes would be fulfilled in and through us.

The fish provided a covering in and from catastrophe. When Jonah was thrown overboard by the mariners, certainly no one thought Jonah would survive. Yet in Jonah's time of personal catastrophe, we see the mercy of God, for God used the fish to provide protection. In judgment, God remembered mercy. Today we still hear testimonies from those whose disobedience brought them to a place where there was no hope of escape, yet God made a way for them, even when their deliverance was not deserved.

The fish provided a change in course. God had called Jonah to go to the city of Nineveh. But he disobeyed and booked passage to Tarshish. Although Jonah had been headed in the wrong direction, the fish God prepared became a vehicle through which

He redirected Jonah's path. When we are truly repentant, God brings forces to bear that will enable us to change our direction. When we are unable to change direction on our own, God will bring about the necessary help so that change can take place. Repentance is always evidenced by a change in direction.

The Gourd

And the Lord God prepared a gourd, and made it to come up over Jonah, that it might be a shadow over his head, to deliver him from his grief. So Jonah was exceeding glad of the gourd (Jonah 4:6).

The gourd provided a chamber of comfort. When Jonah was overcome with heat and ready to faint, the Lord provided a gourd, which shaded Jonah and gave him relief from the hot sun. This was a continuation of God's mercy to Jonah designed to teach him about His forbearance. God pours out His mercy in great measure to saint and sinner alike in order to reveal His goodness.

The gourd provided a contrast of concerns. As Jonah found relief from the sweltering heat, his heart became glad. When a plant, which had no spiritual significance or value, grew up quickly and provided temporary shade, Jonah was happy. On the other hand, when an entire city that had been at the brink of eternal destruction repented, received God's mercy, and was spared, Jonah was displeased and angry. God used the gourd to manifest the misplaced values of Jonah's heart. God desires that His people be concerned with the things that grip His heart. For this reason He allows circumstances to come into our lives that will expose the true intents of our hearts.

The Worm

But God prepared a worm when the morning rose the next day, and it smote the gourd that it withered (Jonah 4:7).

The worm provided chastening for correction. God understood Jonah's conflict with the Ninevites and his struggle to show mercy to a nation he so hated. Therefore, He repeatedly allowed Jonah to be the recipient of great mercy so that he might be touched to change his heart. However, Jonah did not respond to the mercy of God, so God smote the gourd. God desires to reach our hearts through His mercy. But there are times when we fail to respond to His mercy. In times like these, He will use chastisement to bring the needed correction.

The worm provides a collapse of counterfeit comforts. Jonah's values were clearly misplaced. He rejoiced over a plant that had no significance, yet he was not moved over souls that were lost and dying. Therefore God removed what Jonah thought was so important to manifest the futility of his concerns.

The cry of God demonstrates His sovereignty. He can remove what we think is so important in a mere moment of time to show us something of far greater value.

The Vehement East Wind

And it came to pass, when the sun did arise, that God prepared a vehement east wind; and the sun beat upon the head of Jonah, that he fainted, and wished in himself to die, and said, It is better for me to die than to live (Jonah 4:8).

The east wind brings a call for comparison. When God asked Jonah if his anger over the death of the gourd was justified, Jonah declared that he had a right to be angry, even to the point of death (see Jon. 4:9). To this God responded, "You have pity for a gourd for which you did not labor, nor did you make it grow. It grew in a night and perished in a night" (see Jon. 4:10). What was God really doing here? He was showing Jonah the foolishness of temporal values apart from eternal concerns.

The east wind brings a cry for compassion. In one final plea to the heart and mind of Jonah, God asked Jonah, "And should I not spare Nineveh, that great city, wherein are more than sixscore thousand persons that cannot discern between their right hand and their left hand; and also much cattle?" (Jon. 4:11) God's cry to Jonah was a cry of compassion for souls that were lost and dying.

The Book of Jonah offers a marvelous demonstration of God's love and mercy for the lost. In it we find hope for the hopeless—no failure or sin is too great for redemption. We can receive comfort as we listen to the cry of Jonah because we too can use our failures to deliver messages of life to others who are struggling. We too can offer hope to those who have no hope because we once stood where they are now. Let us hear the cry of God's heart as well and rejoice in His everlasting love, for there we will find strength to do His perfect will.

Heavenly Father, our hearts are filled with praise because of Your unfailing mercies toward us. Even when we fail, You are there to restore us. We no longer need to hang our heads in shame because of our sin and disobedience. Rather, we can come to You for forgiveness through the shed blood of the Lord Jesus. We can be restored in Your presence. Help us, Lord, to redeem our failures by rescuing others who struggle as we once did. May our lives be a living demonstration of Your eternal goodness and passion for the world. Amen.

Personal Reflections

When we look at the life of Jonah and the lifestyle of the Ninevites prior to repentance, we are reminded of our own weaknesses, shortcomings, and failures. Like Jonah and the Ninevites, we are confronted with the hopelessness of our mistakes. Consider which of the following characteristics demonstrated in the Book of Jonah that might be present in your own life:

- Self-will
- Disobedience
- Running from God
- Outcast
- Despairing
- Hopelessness
- Headed for destruction

Take Action—Record Your Personal Inventory

1. As you review the above list, what similar feelings do you also share?

2. What caused these feelings to develop?

3. Describe how these feelings interfere with living a victorious Christian life.

4. In what areas has God spoken to you—areas in which you still struggle to obey His purposes for your life?

Take Action—Look for Personal Healing

1. Describe the events that led to Jonah's entombment inside the belly of a fish.

2. Review the scriptural account of Jonah's prayer in which he prayed from the belly of the fish. Note its specific contents as it relates to his deliverance (see Jon. 2).

3. List ways in which you can pray for your restoration.

4. Describe steps you can take that will demonstrate or evidence repentance in your life.

Take Action—Become an Intercessor

1. Name other people you know who also struggle with God's will for their lives.

2. Have you ever made these concerns a matter of prayer? Describe.

3. Examine the prayer of the Ninevites (see Jon. 3:5-10). List important elements in their prayer and behavior that touched the heart of God.

4. Realizing that God is a God of mercy, what could you do and how should you pray in order to bring divine help and restoration for yourself and for others?

Take Action—Reach Out and Help Others

1. In what ways could your triumph become a life-message for others who feel they have hopelessly sinned and are beyond the reach of God?

2. How and where can you share God's mercy on your behalf?

Chapter 4

Nehemiah: A Cry for Rebuilding

That Hanani, one of my brethren, came, he and certain men of Judah; and I asked them concerning the Jews that had escaped, which were left of the captivity, and concerning Jerusalem. And they said unto me, The remnant that are left of the captivity there in the province are in great affliction and reproach: the wall of Jerusalem also is broken down, and the gates thereof are burned with fire. And it came to pass, when I heard these words, that I sat down and wept, and mourned certain days, and fasted, and prayed before the God of heaven (Nehemiah 1:2-4).

> He did not let the weight of his sorrow bring him to the place of collapse. Instead, he was motivated to bring about change.

Two of the most agonizing words people can say are "if only." These words come from the mouths of people to whom life has dealt a terrible blow. Somehow they feel that if they can only undo the mistakes and the misfortunes they've encountered, they would be able to live productive lives in peace. They feel victimized. Their walls of security are broken down, and they no longer feel safe. Unable to cope with their hardships, they remain vulnerable to further destruction. Thank God that His Word offers rebuilding and restoration for the most broken person. There is no situation beyond the help of the Lord. The story of Nehemiah offers a fine example of God's provision of help to people determined to rebuild.

The Scripture passage above relates the cry of Nehemiah, as his heart was breaking for the city and people he loved. The Book of Nehemiah records the sequence of events following the return to Jerusalem. Ezra's ministry focused upon the rebuilding of the temple and the restoration of temple worship. However, the city of Jerusalem still lay in ruin. With its walls broken down, the city and its people remained vulnerable to attack. Nehemiah's burden over their conditions propelled him to a place of intercession and action for the rebuilding of the walls of Jerusalem.

As cupbearer to the king, Nehemiah was responsible for tasting the king's wine before the king would drink. It was a position of great significance and trust, for if anyone tampered with the contents of the wine in an attempt to harm or kill the king, it was Nehemiah who would suffer the consequences instead of the king.

A Cry of Intercession

Born to Jewish parents who were taken as captives to Babylon, Nehemiah had lived his whole life in Babylon. However, he longed to return to Jerusalem, his homeland. When the opportunity presented itself to obtain firsthand information about Jerusalem and its people, Nehemiah met with Hanani (possibly his own brother), an official who directed Jewish affairs in Jerusalem. Nehemiah questioned him regarding the Jewish remnant who had survived exile and the condition of Jerusalem.

Hanani's report was devastating. He told Nehemiah, "...Those who survived the exile and are back in the province are in great trouble and disgrace. The wall of Jerusalem is broken down, and its gates have been burned with fire" (Neh. 1:3 NIV). Hanani's words concerning the conditions of Jerusalem so gripped Nehemiah that he mourned, fasted, and wept for days as he prayed to the Lord (see Neh. 1:4). Nehemiah knew that only divine intervention could bring about change. Therefore He earnestly petitioned God.

...O Lord, God of heaven, the great and awe-some God, who keeps His covenant of love

with those who love Him and obey His commands, let Your ear be attentive and Your eyes open to hear the prayer Your servant is praying before You day and night for Your servants, the people of Israel. I confess the sins we Israelites, including myself and my father's house, have committed against You. We have acted very wickedly toward You. We have not obeyed the commands, decrees and laws You gave Your servant Moses. Remember the instruction You gave Your servant Moses, saying, "If you are unfaithful, I will scatter you among the nations, but if you return to Me and obey My commands, then even if your exiled people are at the farthest horizon, I will gather them from there and bring them to the place I have chosen as a dwelling for My Name." They are Your servants and Your people, whom You redeemed by Your great strength and Your mighty hand. O Lord, let Your ear be attentive to the prayer of this Your servant and to the prayer of Your servants who delight in revering Your name. Give Your servant success today by granting him favor in the presence of this man... (Nehemiah 1:5-11, NIV).

Let us look more closely at some of the principles contained within Nehemiah's prayer:

- He recognized God and His attributes (Neh. 1:5).

- He combined supplication with confession (Neh. 1:6-7).

- He remembered God's promises and past help (Neh. 1:8-11).

- He interceded for divine favor (Neh. 1:11).

Moved to a place of intense sorrow and compassion, Nehemiah became the instrument of God to bring change and restoration. His cry reflected the heart of God. Just as Nehemiah longed to see Jerusalem restored, God longed to see His people restored. Nehemiah shows us an example of godly compassion and intercession. We will benefit from observing Nehemiah's example more closely, for we are often confronted by spiritual ruin and yet somehow fail to be moved by it.

Broken Walls and Burned Gates

God never intended for His people to be taken captive or suffer the hardship of hostile rulership. However, their disobedience to God weakened their defenses. As long as Israel obeyed God, His protection covered them. Their disobedience to His laws removed His hedge of protection.

Symbolically, the walls of Jerusalem stood for *salvation*, and the gates represented *praise*. These are the foundational principles upon which faith operates. (But Thou shalt call Thy walls Salvation, and Thy gates Praise [Is. 60:18b].) When God's principles are neglected, His people become vulnerable to the enemy's attack. When His principles are earnestly followed, the enemy is not able to penetrate God's boundaries of protection. Today countless men and women have become victims of the evils of society and are crying because of their afflictions. Our country was once protected and supported by biblical, foundational truths. Yet sin and rebellion against God have allowed the enemy to make great inroads into our society and break down the walls of protection and truth. Although our country was founded on godly principles, it has drifted far away from its original purposes. Prayer has been removed from our public schools. Humanism has replaced biblical truths. Abortion has been legalized. And our original moral standards based on God's law have been negated, allowing the influx of ungodly lifestyles.

David Barton, in his book *America: To Pray or Not to Pray*[1] charted the specific effects the removal of prayer from public schools[2] had in students, parents, education, and the nation. The results were astonishing. The charts and graphs he provides

---

1. David Barton, *America: To Pray or Not to Pray* (Aledo: WallBuilder Press, 1994).
2. June 25, 1962, *Engel v. Vitale.*

clearly demonstrate marked deterioration that began the year following the removal of prayer and of God from schools. SAT scores plummeted. Sharp and continuous increases spiraled upward in many troubled areas. The following list mentions just a few of these areas that showed dramatic increase and have been significant national problems since the 1962 U.S. Supreme Court decision to remove prayer from our schools:

- Premarital sexual activity among U.S. teens
- Teen pregnancy
- Sexually transmitted diseases
- Student suicide
- Illegal drug use
- Youth runaways
- School dropouts
- School violence
- Alcohol consumption
- Divorce
- Child abuse

These tragic problem areas together with the lack of moral foundation and stability in our schools and society have left our country in a state of spiritual ruin. Walls of protection have been torn down. Doors have been opened wide for enemy infiltration.

More Than Sorrow Needed to Bring About Change

Nehemiah's personal cry also communicated the corporate cry of a people who had suffered the privation of captivity and loss. God's people were defenseless—completely open to the onslaughts of their enemies. Although two other groups of exiles had returned to Jerusalem years earlier—the first group led by Zerubbabel in 538 B.C. and the second group led by Ezra in 458 B.C.—the walls of the city remained broken. Returning to Jerusalem was not enough to bring restoration to a city that lay in ruin. What the Jews needed most was leadership. Many felt sorrowful about the existing conditions. However, sorrow alone could not bring change.

Nehemiah did not run from his sorrow; rather he embraced it. In so doing, he allowed sorrow to work for him. With the help of the Holy Spirit, he interceded for his people. Nehemiah cried out to God for a corporate need. He did not let the weight of his sorrow bring him to the place of collapse. Instead, he was motivated to bring about change. With insight and godly wisdom, he provided exactly what was needed to bring about restoration. He gave direction, leadership, and action.

A Plan of Action

Because Nehemiah did not let grief paralyze his steps, nor did he let the enormity of the problem prohibit involvement, he was able to formulate a plan for restoration. He gave his talents to God. God used Nehemiah's natural intellect as well as his spiritual abilities. His steps were well planned and properly executed.

1. He petitioned the king for a leave (Neh. 2:5-8).

2. He made an assessment of the damages (Neh. 2:13-17).

3. He did not disclose his plan prematurely (Neh. 2:12,16).

4. He motivated others and organized them to help (Neh. 2:17-18).

5. He developed strategy appropriate to the conflict (Neh. 3).

6. He continued in the face of opposition (Neh. 4).

7. He finished the work God called him to do (Neh. 6:15).

Coming Against the Enemy

Nehemiah encountered many problems as he gave himself to the task of rebuilding the walls. Repeatedly, the enemy tried to defeat him and stop the work. But instead of giving up, Nehemiah forged ahead. As the need arose, he reorganized his workers. Some of his workers, weapons in hand, stood guard to protect the laborers who worked on the wall. Prayer accompanied their every step.

Nehemiah continually encouraged his workers, reminding them that God was with them. With each new attack from their enemies, Nehemiah responded with prayer and then took appropriate action. Nehemiah did not quit but continued until the job was done.

With the rebuilding of the walls of Jerusalem also came the re-establishment of worship. Evidence of revival was clearly demonstrated, as was a new unity among the people. They all gathered together as one man, eager to hear God's Word. Earnestly they came before Ezra to hear him present the law of Moses. He read the words of life to them from the morning until midday. Their attention was focused. And as he read, their hearts opened before the Lord. Without exception, all the people lifted up their hands toward heaven and bowed their heads as they worshiped. They continued to listen with contrite hearts. "Mourn not, nor weep" they were instructed, "for the joy of the Lord is your strength" (see Neh. 8:10). The hearts of the people rejoiced as they understood the wonderful words of life. God's Spirit continued to work mightily among them, and further evidences of revival emerged as they obeyed God's precepts, confessed their sins, and separated themselves unto the Lord.

A Result of Victory

Nehemiah's achievement in rebuilding the walls of Jerusalem in 52 days in the face of such overwhelming hindrances can provide hope and inspiration to us today. God enabled teams of people to work energetically and consistently until they reached the place of victory. Through their example we can be assured that when we also seek to repair broken standards and restore godly principles, God will bring His unlimited resources to our assistance. He will do whatever it takes to give us victory. He will place the right people before us at just the right time to encourage and support us. He will help us to overcome impossible circumstances. He will make a way where no way exists. Once we accomplish the task of rebuilding, God will graciously pour out His Holy Spirit upon us in great measure.

Heavenly Father, we confess that we are broken and in need of Your healing. You alone can rebuild all the damaged areas of our lives. Your love and mercy are the only answers to our pain. We realize that some of our brokenness is because of our own neglect, and for that we ask Your forgiveness. Some of our sorrows are because we have been victims of the evils of our day, and for that we ask for a Holy Ghost revival. We pray for Your Spirit to bring conviction and change. Quicken us that we might be catalysts for Your divine purposes. Amen.

Personal Reflections

A study of Nehemiah and the conditions of Jerusalem provide clear insight into some of the problems that plague society today. It reminds us of the many people who are not only vulnerable to the attack of the enemy but have succumbed to defeat because of the brokenness in their lives. Truths and values have been negated that were once held dear. Parents who once tenaciously guarded their homes have now abandoned their responsibilities. We recognize patterns of destruction everywhere:

- Broken relationships with God
- Destruction of foundational truths
- Broken relationships with families
- Absence of godly support systems
- Helplessness and desperation
- Vulnerability to greater harm and destruction
- No signs of improvement or change

Take Action—Record Your Personal Inventory

1. As you review the above list, which of these circumstances do you see affecting your own life?
2. What events caused these conditions in your home?

3. Describe how these problems contribute to feelings of vulnerability.

4. As you examine your failures or the failures of those you know and love, what reasons would you list as responsible for the lack of victory or change?

Take Action—Look for Personal Healing

1. Many people felt sorrowful over the plight of Jerusalem, but sorrow alone could not bring change. How did Nehemiah handle his sorrow?

2. How did sorrow work for good in Nehemiah's life?

3. Describe how God can use sorrow to motivate you to the place of healing.

4. Through gleaning principles for change from the example of Nehemiah, what course of action could you take that would also bring change?

Take Action—Become an Intercessor

1. Name other people you know who share similar circumstances to your own.

2. Have you ever made these concerns a matter of prayer? Describe.

3. Review the scriptural account of Nehemiah's prayer as he cried out for his people. Note its

specific contents as it relates to intercession (see Neh. 1:4-11). How can you also intercede for restoration?

Take Action—Reach Out and Help Others

1. Nehemiah knew it would take more than sorrow to bring about change. With the help of God, he devised a plan of action that brought restoration to a people who had suffered loss for many years. In what ways could your triumph be translated into action on behalf of those who cry as you once did?

2. Examine where God has placed you and describe how God can use you as a catalyst for change.

Chapter 5

Esther: A Cry
for a New Covenant

Then Queen Esther answered, "If I have found
favor with you, O king, and if it pleases your
majesty, grant me my life—this is my petition.
And spare my people—this is my request. For
I and my people have been sold for destruc-
tion and slaughter and annihilation. If we
had merely been sold as male and female
slaves, I would have kept quiet, because no
such distress would justify disturbing the
king." ... *"For how can I bear to see disaster fall*
on my people? How can I bear to see the de-
struction of my family?" (Esther 7:3; 8:6 NIV)

We can hear in the personal cry of Esther
the corporate cry of a people who desperately needed a way of salvation even
when no way had previously existed.

Every so often in the news, we hear of civic leaders campaigning relentlessly for the rights of criminals awaiting the death penalty. They are determined to get the convict's death sentence commuted by whatever legal means are at their disposal. The efforts of these leaders are not supported by everyone; there are those who feel that through execution criminals are receiving what they deserve. In the story of Esther we find the example of an entire people who are condemned to death. Although they were entirely innocent of any crime or wrongdoing, the decree for their execution had been signed by the king without leaving any possibility for reprieve or alteration.

The Scripture passage quoted earlier relates the agonizing cry of Esther as she pleaded with her husband the king to spare the lives of the Jewish people throughout the land. The devil intended to destroy God's people through this grave plot, but through intercession, the power of God suddenly changed the planned course of events.

The Book of Esther depicts some of the conditions surrounding God's people during their exile in Persia. Esther, a Jew, was chosen to be queen of the land by the providence of God. She replaced Queen Vashti, who was removed as queen because of her disobedience to a direct order from her husband, King Ahasuerus. Vashti was unwilling to be put on display as a showpiece before men and the kingdom.

Her disobedience incurred the wrath of the king and he divorced her.

Esther was an orphan raised by her older cousin Mordecai. They were living in Shushan as a result of the Babylonian captivity of Israel. Word began to circulate that the king was looking for a new bride. In order to select the most beautiful wife, he held a "beauty contest." It was through this contest that Esther was chosen as the new queen.

A Plot to Destroy the Jews

Mordecai was a God-fearing Jew who worked as a government official. His place of employment enabled him to continue a close relationship with Esther even while she reigned as queen. In the time of crisis, Mordecai was able to unburden his heart to his cousin. He told her about the wicked plot that had been devised by Haman, a self-serving official who was second-in-command in the empire. Haman was an Agagite—a race of ancient enemies of the Jews. When Mordecai refused to bow in reverence to him, Haman became enraged. At that moment, he began to look for a way to kill Mordecai. Later at the suggestion of his wife and all his friends, he constructed gallows on which he planned to hang Mordecai. He also planned to destroy all Jews living within the boundaries of Persia. In order to carry out his wicked plot, Haman deceived the king. He manipulated him into signing an edict that singled the Jews out for total destruction.

..."There is a certain people dispersed and scattered among the peoples in all the provinces of your kingdom whose customs are different from those of all other people and who do not obey the king's laws; it is not in the king's best interest to tolerate them. If it please the king, let a decree be issued to destroy them, and I will put ten thousand talents of silver into the royal treasury for the men who carry out this business" (Esther 3:8-9 NIV).

We might think that Haman's financial offer to the king should have made the king suspicious of what unstated motives Haman had. The average income of a Persian official was about 15,000 talents a year. Therefore, when Haman offered the king 10,000 talents, he was offering two-thirds of his annual salary. It also could have been considered strange that these efforts, purported to be in the interest of the king's protection, would be funded by the efforts of one citizen rather than the reserves of the royal treasury. Yet the king trusted Haman's words and gave him the authority to write up and send out the decree he desired.

A Call for Involvement

When Haman's intentions became known to Mordecai, he "cried with a loud and a bitter cry" (Esther 4:1). Esther, hearing news of his mourning, sent a servant to Mordecai in order to find out what was going on. Mordecai told her of the impending doom. He then entreated her to go before the king and make supplication for her people. He further reminded her that if she failed to plead for mercy, she and her father's house would also perish. Therefore, Esther began to prepare herself to cry out to the king to spare the lives of her people. Esther's cry represented the cry of all the Jews doomed for destruction. By petitioning the king, Esther was pleading for their deliverance.

A Call for Intercession

Esther was keenly aware that only divine intervention could change the intended course of events. Therefore, she formulated a plan to fast and pray for three days along with her staff and all the Jews who lived in the city. So consumed was she with her mission, she was willing to lay her life down on behalf of the people she loved.

Go, gather together all the Jews that are present in Shushan, and fast ye for me, and neither eat nor drink three days, night or day: I also and my maidens will fast likewise; and so will I go in unto the king, which is not according to the law: and if I perish, I perish (Esther 4:16).

A Plan for a Godly Appeal

In order to make intercession to the king, Esther carefully planned the way in which she would approach him. Her plan was skillfully executed with the preparation of two banquets for just two guests—the king and Haman. With a display of grace and gentleness, she established rapport, paving the way for a godly appeal.

The real turning point of this story, however, takes place in what appears to be rather trivial coincidences. Between the two banquets, the king was unable to sleep. Therefore, he commanded that the court annals be read to him. It was during this reading that the king learned how Mordecai spared his life five years earlier by foiling an assassination attempt. He also learned that Mordecai was not rewarded for this act of kindness. With a twist of irony and unusual timing, Haman suddenly walked into the king's outer court. Haman's intention was to speak with the king about his plans to hang Mordecai. But before he could speak to the king on this matter, the king asked him, "What should be done unto the man whom the king delights to honor?"

Haman assumed that he was the man the king wished to honor. Therefore, he outlined a lavish plan. When posing his question, the king unintentionally kept from Haman the identity of "the man whom the king delighteth to honour" (Esther 6:6). However, earlier Haman had intentionally withheld from the king the identity of the "certain people scattered abroad" whom he felt the king should destroy (Esther 3:8). One could only imagine the anger and grief Haman felt when he was required to bestow upon Mordecai the honor he coveted for himself.

During the second banquet, Esther told the king of Haman's wicked plot to destroy the Jews. The king reacted with swift and final judgment. Haman was hanged on the very gallows he had built for Mordecai.

So they hanged Haman on the gallows that he had prepared for Mordecai. Then was the king's wrath pacified (Esther 7:10).

Esther knew it would take more than a burden to bring about victory. With encouragement from Mordecai and an anointing from God, she devised a plan that brought great deliverance to her and her people. Let us review the steps Esther took:

1. She grieved over the wrongdoing of others (Esther 4:4).

2. She inquired to know the facts (Esther 4:5).

3. She received a commission for the necessity of her involvement (Esther 4:8).

4. She received a word of wisdom (Esther 4:14).

5. She responded to crisis with a call for intercession (Esther 4:16).

6. She was fully dedicated to her mission (Esther 4:16).

7. She took action following intercession (Esther 5:1).

8. She used grace and gentleness as powerful tools (Esther 5:2).

9. She developed a rapport with her audience before speaking her mind (Esther 5:4).

10. She proceeded with caution, thereby increasing the curiosity of others as to her purpose (Esther 5:8).

11. At the appropriate time, she spoke right to the heart of the matter (Esther 7:3).

12. She identified the problem to the one who could bring change (Esther 7:6).

13. She did not rest with partial victory (Esther 8:3).

14. She saw the fruit of her travail (Esther 8:11; 9:5).

A Cry for Reversal

Esther did not rest or become content with partial victory. Haman's execution was not enough. The previous edict, signed by the king and sealed with his ring, still remained. It still declared that the Jews would be slaughtered. According to Persian law, once an edict was signed and sealed by the king, it could not be revoked. In the wake of this dilemma there was only one solution: A new law had to be written that would overtake the provision of the old law. In response to Esther's cry, the king granted permission for this new law to be written. Therefore, the Jews were given permission to rise up in self-defense and destroy their enemies on the very same day they themselves were to be destroyed.

Wherein the king granted the Jews which were in every city to gather themselves together, and to stand for their life, to destroy, to slay, and to cause to perish, all the power of the people and province that would assault them, both little ones and women, and to take the spoil of them for a prey (Esther 8:11).

A Cry for a New Covenant

The symbolism contained within this narrative is so powerful. The first law that the king had signed and sealed with his ring—a law that would have destroyed God's people—represented the Old Covenant. The new law that the king had written to reverse the provisions of the first law represented the New Covenant.

The Old Covenant declared, *"The soul that sinneth, it shall die"* (Ezek. 18:20). God's written and spoken law pronounced judgment and destruction for all sinners. There was no way to revoke the existing law. Without cancellation, God's people were doomed. The New Covenant declared, *"whosoever believeth in Him should not perish, but have eternal life"* (Jn. 3:15).

We can hear in the personal cry of Esther the corporate cry of a people who desperately needed a way of salvation even when no way had previously existed. When Esther cried out for a new law to put away the determinations of the old law, she cried out prophetically for the whole Church of God. It was a cry for the Old Covenant to be overtaken with a New Covenant. The Old Covenant declared destruction, but the New Covenant pronounced life.

Christ hath redeemed us from the curse of the law, being made a curse for us: for it is written, Cursed is every one that hangeth on a tree: ... To redeem them that were under the law, that we might receive the adoption of sons (Galatians 3:13; 4:5).

There is therefore now no condemnation to them which are in Christ Jesus, who walk not after the flesh, but after the Spirit. For the law of the Spirit of life in Christ Jesus hath made me free from the law of sin and death (Romans 8:1-2).

Heavenly Father, when we were lost and helpless, You found a way to save us. No longer do we groan as those without hope. Our inability to keep the law can no longer be held as a snare to defeat us. With triumph we look to the finished work of Christ. There we see our Savior who kept a law we could not keep, and because of Your mercy, His righteousness is imputed to our account. We thank You for His shed blood, which provided a new covenant and gave us new life. Amen.

Personal Reflections

When we examine the plight of the Jewish people who were exiles along with Esther in a foreign land, we readily see similarities that have engulfed all of us. We are confronted with the hardship of sin's captivity and the hopelessness of our rescue. We are...

- Victims of sin's captivity
- Victims of society's failures
- Hopelessly facing destruction
- Bound by a law we cannot keep
- Doomed by a law we cannot change
- Unable to plead in our own behalf
- Consumed with a cry of bitterness

Fortunately, Jesus Christ has provided for our help in our every need. His work on the cross accomplished what we could never have achieved on our own. In Him is restoration, healing, and hope.

Take Action—Record Your Personal Inventory

1. As you take spiritual stock of yourself, starting with the inward man, what similar feelings and characteristics do you share with the exiles of Persia?

2. To what causes do you attribute responsibility for the conditions in which you find yourself?

3. How do your circumstances prevent you from living joyously?

4. What attempts have you made to achieve victory, and how have they failed?

Take Action—Look for Personal Healing

1. In what ways did God use Esther's impending doom as a means of victory?

2. Review the steps Esther took that brought a great deliverance to her and her people. Name some of the important steps that contributed to her victory.

3. Why did Esther and her maidens fast for three days before she took any action?

4. Ask the Holy Spirit to show you how to pray and what steps you also can take to receive victory in your life.

Take Action—Become an Intercessor

1. How many other people do you know who are also in desperate circumstances? Name some who are close to you.

2. How often do you pray for the needs and problems of those you love who share your struggles? Describe the way you pray for these needs.

3. In what ways was Esther an intercessor for her people?

4. Describe ways you also can be an intercessor.

Take Action—Reach Out and Help Others

1. In what ways could your understanding and experience in New Covenant relationship with Jesus bring hope to those who struggle under the Old Covenant?

2. Describe the benefits of a support system and how it can help others achieve the victory you now enjoy.

Chapter 6

Hannah: A Cry for Fulfillment

And she was in bitterness of soul, and prayed unto the Lord, and wept sore. And she vowed a vow, and said, O Lord of hosts, if Thou wilt indeed look on the affliction of Thine handmaid, and remember me, and not forget Thine handmaid, but wilt give unto Thine handmaid a man child, then I will give him unto the Lord all the days of his life, and there shall no razor come upon his head. And it came to pass, as she continued praying before the Lord, that Eli marked her mouth. Now Hannah, she spake in her heart; only her lips moved, but her voice was not heard: therefore Eli thought she had been drunken. And Eli said unto her, How long wilt thou be drunken? put away thy wine from thee. And Hannah answered and said, No, my lord, I am a woman of a sorrowful spirit: I have drunk neither wine nor strong drink, but have poured out my soul before the Lord (1 Samuel 1:10-15).

> We hear in the anguish of Hannah's cry, the cry of the empty womb.

We live in a marvelous era of great technology. Working together, doctors and scientists are accomplishing feats that were once thought impossible. Women unable to conceive by traditional means are able to do so through in vitro fertilization. More than a dozen years ago, it was major headline news to read about "test-tube babies." How did this come about? What impetus drove doctors to such depths of exploration and experimentation? It was the intense cries of women longing for fulfillment through motherhood. For these women, their destiny and hope for the future was wrapped up in children yet unborn.

In this passage we have the cry of Hannah—the agonizing cry of a barren wife. According to ancient Middle Eastern custom, it was a reproach for a married woman to go childless. In fact, she was considered a failure in her role as a woman if she did not produce children. She became a social embarrassment to her husband, who was even permitted to use her barrenness as grounds for divorce. In this narrative, however, Hannah's husband Elkanah chose to remain with her and lovingly cared for her.

Adding to her grief was the ridicule she endured from Peninnah, Elkanah's other wife.

And her adversary also provoked her sore, for to make her fret, because the Lord had shut up her womb (1 Samuel 1:6).

Unable to Rejoice

All Israelite men were required to attend religious feasts held at the temple three times each year. In keeping with this custom, Elkanah and his family made their journey to Shiloh to offer sacrifices unto the Lord. At a time when others were feasting and rejoicing before the Lord because of His blessings, Hannah was broken by her personal sorrow and anguish. Her grief was obvious to her husband who commented to her, "Don't I mean more to you than ten sons?" Unable to contain her sorrow, Hannah cried out in "bitterness of soul." There in the temple, she wept and prayed to the Lord. The intensity of her feelings were manifested through her actions: She wept greatly, refused to eat, experienced bitterness of soul, felt forgotten by God, and had a sorrowful spirit (see 1 Sam. 1:7-11).

In spite of Hannah's struggles and negative feelings, her prayer contains important principles regarding the ministry of intercession.

1. She had a great sense of need (1 Sam. 1:6-7).

2. She prayed with earnestness (1 Sam. 1:10).

3. She directed her prayers to the Lord (1 Sam. 1:10).

4. She dedicated the answer unto the Lord (1 Sam. 1:11).

5. She prayed with importunity (1 Sam. 1:12).

6. She prayed until she had assurance (1 Sam. 1:17).

The Cry of the Empty Womb

In the anguish of Hannah's cry we hear the cry of the empty womb. That which was made for reproduction and life was empty and barren. Month after month, her body went through cycles of preparation, longing for conception that did not occur. With each passing month and each passing year, the disappointment of being unfulfilled grew.

Words That Bring Defeat

It is not difficult to imagine Hannah's feelings of despair as she struggled with childlessness. Her disappointment, longing, and other negative feelings were no doubt further aggravated by the words she heard from others. Altogether she seemed to be facing an insurmountable obstacle of personal defeat.

So often when things appear to go wrong, there are those who are quick to respond with words of judgment or rebuke, "What sin did she commit that caused this problem?" Even if words are never spoken, there will still be those who silently wonder, "What did she do that brought the judgment of God upon her life?" There is something in human nature that finds it so easy to point a judgmental finger. It is so easy to be a "Job's comforter" and offer all kinds of theories and speculations as to what went wrong and why. Well meaning Christians often become caught up in giving unsolicited advice—advice that brings more hurt than comfort.

Perhaps even worse than the jeers of onlookers are the words of accusations we speak to ourselves while we struggle with our conflicts. Unable to understand the misfortunes that befall us, we are convinced that either we or our parents must have sinned and thus caused the judgment of God to come upon us. Our personal commentaries become a rehearsal of personal failures. Unable to satisfy our unanswered questions, we invent meaningless explanations that drive ourselves into deeper and deeper despair.

Misunderstood by Those in Ministry

As if Hannah's grief wasn't enough, it was further compounded by the misunderstanding of Eli the priest. He observed her weeping before the Lord, praying in her heart, her lips moving without uttering a single word aloud. Eli assumed she was drunk. His rebuke brought her reply:

"Not so, my lord," Hannah replied, "I am a woman who is deeply troubled. I have not been drinking wine or beer; I was pouring out my soul to the Lord. Do not take your servant for a wicked woman; I have been praying here out of my great anguish and grief" (1 Samuel 1:15-16 NIV).

Eli was quick to respond with words of comfort, "Go in peace, and may the God of Israel grant you what you have asked of Him" (1 Sam. 1:17 NIV). Hannah immediately accepted Eli's words as an answer from God. She put away her sorrow and continued about her business.

The Cry for Fruitfulness

Although Hannah may not have been consciously aware of all the dealings of God and how He desired to use her to bring forth His purposes, her cry was really prompted by God. What she saw in the natural—a desire for a "man child"—God saw in the spiritual. For Hannah, the cry of the empty womb was a cry for fruitfulness. She was longing to see the purposes of God fulfilled in and through her. It was a cry to bring forth Samuel—an arrow of the Lord that would pierce the spiritual darkness surrounding Israel. It was a cry for God's purposes to come forth. It was a cry for significance that would extend beyond the years of her lifetime. Through her seed, arrows of truth would be launched beyond the borders of her reach.

God put that cry within Hannah. He knew He could find in her a willing and yielded vessel. Note the two-sided purpose in her cry:

1. Hannah longed for a child.
2. God longed for a servant through whom He could speak righteousness to a backslidden nation.

There are times God may call us to prayer or intercession, and our understanding of what God wants to do in and through us may be limited. God may have a much broader purpose in mind when we may see it touching just one area. Without knowing or understanding the mind of the Lord, we can often fail to press through. Therefore, it is important that we be quick to obey the prompting of the Lord. I am convinced there are times God uses us for His glory and we remain unaware of the full impact of what He has accomplished through us. God looks for people who will work jointly with Him, consciously and unconsciously toward the achievement of His ultimate purposes.

Lo, children are an heritage of the Lord: and the fruit of the womb is his reward. As arrows are in the hand of a mighty man; so are children of the youth. Happy is the man that hath his quiver full of them: they shall not be ashamed, but they shall speak with the enemies in the gate (Psalm 127:3-5).

The Cry of a Barren Nation

Contained within the personal cry of Hannah was the corporate cry of a nation that was spiritually barren and unfulfilled. Israel had drifted from the purposes of God. Once Israel had been a theocratic nation, living under the rulership of God. Now the priesthood was no longer a place of God's anointing. Eli the high priest along with his two sons, also priests of the Lord, brought corruption and disgrace to the name of God. Hannah's cry contains a cry against religious corruption—corruption within the ministry. The misplaced priorities of Eli's family is clearly demonstrated by the following words of the Lord:

Why do you scorn My sacrifice and offering that I prescribed for My dwelling? Why do you honor your sons more than Me by fattening yourselves on the choice parts of every offering made by My people Israel? (1 Samuel 2:29 NIV).

For I have told [Eli] *that I will judge his house for ever for the iniquity which he knoweth; because his sons made themselves vile, and he restrained them not* (1 Samuel 3:13).

For Eli and his sons, the ministry was dishonored because they looked for personal gain rather than sacrificial living. They disregarded the prescribed method by which offerings and sacrifices to the Lord were to be handled. And they fattened themselves on the most desirable parts of every offering made by the people. So entrenched were they with their selfish greed, they refused any form of correction. God's standards of holiness were neglected and negated by their loose living. Israel along with its priests had fallen prey to moral decay.

Eli knew his sons were living in sin, but he did nothing about it. In fact, even warnings from the Lord that judgment would come upon his house did not move him to rebuke or restrain his sons from their contemptible behavior. Eli failed as a parent because he failed to bring correction to his own children. Eli failed as a priest because he did not offer spiritual life to the people of God. Like those before him, Eli contributed to the barrenness of the nation. Israel had only a form of godliness; they lacked the demonstration of the power of God. Outwardly, they demonstrated to the world a religious practice without experiencing any inward reality: "Having a form of godliness, but denying the power thereof..." (2 Tim. 3:5).

The Cry of an Intercessor

Only true intercessors so identify with the problem for which they pray that they are willing for the answer to be brought through them. Israel needed a mighty man of God to bring restoration. Through her prayer Hannah willingly offered both herself and the child for whom she prayed to God for His purpose. Hannah's cry was also a cry for a prophetic move of God. It was a cry that ushered in the prophetic voice of Samuel, establishing holiness and righteousness without compromise.

> ..."*O Lord Almighty, if You will only look upon Your servant's misery and remember me, and not forget Your servant but give her a son, then I will give him to the Lord for all the days of his life, and no razor will ever be used on his head*" (1 Samuel 1:11 NIV).

Hannah was willing to bear the burden of the Lord for Israel's desperate need. She was to offer her womb to carry His purposes and to travail in birth until the life of God came forth and brought restoration to a barren nation.

A Satisfied Mother in Israel

Hannah willingly offered to the Lord the child for which she prayed. No doubt this was a costly commitment, yet she did it without hesitation. Hannah was filled with joy that she could freely give back to God that which He had loaned. She was so filled with the Spirit of God at the dedication of her child to the Lord that she began to prophesy mightily and declare the goodness and sovereignty of God. It is no wonder that Samuel was destined to become a great prophet of God.

As a mother in Israel, Hannah's personal cry contained the corporate cry of her nation. Therefore, the fulfillment of her cry was also the fulfillment for a nation. Hannah's cry was much more than a cry for children. It was a cry to make herself available to God that He might bring renewal through her. Within her cry was the recognition of a need and a willingness to be part of the solution.

The Cry of a Barren Church

For too long the Church has remained barren, fruitless, and unfulfilled in its mission. The empty womb of the Church desires fulfillment through the purpose of God and is crying out. That which was meant for life and reproduction has only been going through the motions, holding service after service without any real manifestation of the life of God. Life can only come forth when people give themselves as Hannah did to carry the burden of the Lord. There must be those who are willing to travail in labor until they bring forth life and restoration within the Church. The prophetic move of God will sweep away the lethargy and corruption brought by sin.

For as soon as Zion travailed, she brought forth her children (Isaiah 66:8c).

The Cry of the Godly

Hannah's story offers hope to all who struggle in this manner. Hannah was clearly a godly woman of great integrity. Yet in her example we see that godliness is not a protection from personal sorrow. Neither are hardships or misfortunes indicators of sin or wrongdoing. We learn some lessons through our pain that we cannot learn any other way. God wants to bring forth a life through us that cannot come out unless we go through the difficulties He permits to fall across our path. As we offer up our struggles in intercession for those who struggle, we can bring hope and life to others.

Heavenly Father, in our barrenness we come to You. You have a plan that exceeds our struggles. May our cry for fulfillment be a longing to see Your purposes accomplished in and through us. In Your great wisdom You have allowed our pain in order that we might call upon Your name. Help us to be responsive to the workings of Your Spirit. We offer ourselves to You and pray that Your life through us would bring healing and restoration to those in need. Bring revival to our churches and to our land. Amen.

Personal Reflections

We can easily relate to the cry of Hannah when we think of all the people we know, perhaps even ourselves, who wander aimlessly through life—going through the motions but never finding fulfillment or purpose. Without an attachment of significance to our lives, we will experience barrenness. There are many for whom life holds no meaning, and like Hannah, they cry out in their desire for fulfillment. For some persons, the feelings of emptiness are suppressed or camouflaged in a flood of activities. In other persons, these feelings are readily apparent. The following list identifies some key symptoms of a lack of fulfillment in life:

- Lack of vibrant relationship with Jesus Christ
- Lack of significant relationship with others
- Lack of purpose
- Lack of job satisfaction
- Lack of enthusiasm for daily activities
- Lack of connection with a local church
- Lack of joy

Take Action—Record Your Personal Inventory

1. As you review the above list, what similar feelings or situations do you share?

2. List the causes you consider to be responsible for the areas of lack in your life.

3. How is the lack of satisfaction manifested in your life?

4. What activities do you use to hide your emptiness?

Take Action—Look for Personal Healing

1. In what ways did God use Hannah's sorrow to bring about His divine purposes?

2. Review Hannah's prayer (see 1 Sam. 1:6-18). Do you think she was aware of God's ultimate plan for her life?

3. List ways that you can pray in order to bring personal healing.

4. Describe ways in which you can demonstrate faith toward God even before you see the answer to your prayers.

Take Action—Become an Intercessor

1. Name other people you know who also struggle with lack of purpose or fulfillment.

2. Have you ever asked the Holy Spirit to burden your heart so that you can pray for these needs? Describe.

3. As we study Hannah's cry, we realize that she was prompted by the Holy Spirit to bring about God's purposes He had stirred within

her. If you were to take spiritual inventory of churches with which you are acquainted, how could you pray and intercede for God to bring spiritual renewal?

Take Action—Reach Out and Help Others

1. Describe how your answered prayers and God's ultimate purposes for you and the Body of Christ can bring hope and excitement to those in need.

2. In what ways and to whom can you demonstrate God's victory?

Chapter 7

David: A Cry for Intimacy With God

My soul longeth, yea, even fainteth for the courts of the Lord: my heart and my flesh crieth out for the living God (Psalm 84:2).

As the hart panteth after the water brooks, so panteth my soul after Thee, O God. My soul thirsteth for God, for the living God: when shall I come and appear before God? My tears have been my meat day and night, while they continually say unto me, Where is thy God? When I remember these things, I pour out my soul in me: for I had gone with the multitude, I went with them to the house of God, with the voice of joy and praise, with a multitude that kept holyday. Why art thou cast down, O my soul? And why art thou disquieted in me? hope thou in God: for I shall yet praise Him for the help of His countenance. O my God,

*my soul is cast down within me: therefore will
I remember Thee from the land of Jordan,
and of the Hermonites, from the hill Mizar.
Deep calleth unto deep at the noise of Thy waterspouts: all Thy waves and Thy billows are
gone over me* (Psalm 42:1-7).

**The only cry that could bring change was
the cry for the living God.**

The confessions of Saint Augustine display the
marvelous truth of man's longing for God. Prior to
his encounter with God, Saint Augustine lived
recklessly, not knowing or caring about God.
Although he searched for truth through various
philosophies, he remained disillusioned and unsat-
isfied until the truth of God's Word found lodging in
his heart. His mother prayed for his conversion for
18 years. Then one glorious day, he experienced the
reality of a personal encounter with God, and his life
was dramatically changed. No longer alone or empty,
his life became filled with purpose as he walked with
God. In his autobiography, he declared with
profound insight, "For Thou has made us for Thyself
and our hearts are restless till they rest in Thee."[1]
Augustine's experience with God convinced him
that man was created by God and for God and within
the heart of man is a vacuum that can only be filled

---

1. *Confessions of Saint Augustine* (Sheed and Ward, 1943;
Scranton, PA: Hadden Craftsmen, Inc.).

by God. This is the universal cry of man; it is a cry for intimacy with God.

Throughout the Book of Psalms we are given repeated glimpses into the many cries of the psalmists—David, the descendants of Korah, and others. We find the real David in the Book of Psalms, the one who pours his soul out to God. We are touched, not by David's greatness, but by his weakness. We are moved, not by his kingship, but by his dependency upon God. We relate to the psalms because in their words we see our own hearts. In the cries of David we recognize our deepest cries. And along with David we realize that only God can satisfy our deepest longings.

David's experience ranged from obscure shepherd boy to king of Israel. Between these two extremes, we see a young man with a heart after God. He often mused over the goodness of the Lord and gave musical expression to the feelings of his heart. During one period of his life he was also on the run for his life, hotly pursued by his enemies. Even in these dark days, he cried out to the Lord and glorified God for His help and faithfulness.

A Thirst for God

In the passages we read at the start of this chapter, we hear in the psalmists' cries a longing for a living relationship with God. Although these two psalms (Psalms 42 and 84) were probably written by the sons of Korah, I have taken the liberty of including them here because they so completely capture the spirit David himself expressed. (David had appointed men from the descendants of Korah to serve in the temple as choir leaders. They continued to serve as Levitical musicians for hundreds of years.) The words of these psalmists reveal an intense cry from the very depths of their hearts, one that permeated every fiber of their beings—the soul, heart, and flesh.

Psalm 42 describes a scene of intense thirst, a deer panting after a water brook. The psalmist knew well that animals and even people can go for prolonged periods without food but certainly not without water. Intense thirst can drive both people and animals to extremes in their search for satisfaction. Thus so the writer of Psalm 42 cried out in longing and in anguish, knowing that for him life could not continue unless his thirst for God was satisfied. (It is interesting to note that a deer would also seek a water brook when hotly pursued by its enemy. Immersed within the safety of its waters, the deer's scent becomes lost to the enemy.)

David also expressed the same intense thirsting for God in Psalm 63 when he states, "O God, Thou art my God; early will I seek Thee: my soul thirsteth for Thee, my flesh longeth for Thee in a dry and thirsty land, where no water is" (verse 1). In Psalm 143 David repeats this same thought, "I stretch forth my hands unto Thee: my soul thirsteth after Thee, as a thirsty land..." (verse 6).

I know that my life on the East Coast of the United States has prevented me from fully appreciating the powerful descriptions of these psalms. I am used to seeing lush green fields. I take for granted the vast array of plants and flowers that freely grow in the well watered areas around me. However, on a recent trip to the Arizona desert, I was reminded of what a "dry and thirsty land" really was. As I exited the airport terminal, my eyes fell on the brown, parched ground. I didn't see grass anywhere. I was deeply impressed by the dryness around me. That scene became permanently etched into my mind. Not only was the ground dry and barren, but everywhere I looked the soil was cracked and split. It was as if the ground itself was crying out for water. My mind came back to these verses. I heard myself cry with David, "My soul thirsteth for Thee, my flesh longeth for Thee in a dry and thirsty land, where no water is."

Remembering God and Longing for His Presence

There were times when David was unable to go to the temple of the Lord because he was in hiding, a hunted man. King Saul, consumed with jealousy, often sought to kill him. During these times David reflected on his previous experiences with the Lord and found new strength.

My soul shall be satisfied as with marrow and fatness; and my mouth shall praise Thee with joyful lips: when I remember Thee upon my bed, and meditate on Thee in the night watches. Because Thou hast been my help, therefore in the shadow of Thy wings will I rejoice (Psalm 63:5-7).

Once David tasted of the goodness and the presence of the Lord, he could not do without it. His appetite was stirred and quickened. An inward hunger arose for a conscious, vibrant encounter with God. The apostle Peter in his first Epistle expresses a very similar thought, "Like newborn babies, crave pure spiritual milk, so that by it you may grow up in your salvation, now that you have tasted that the Lord is good" (1 Pet. 2:2-3 NIV). For David, the awareness of God's presence was the satisfaction that the "King of glory" had come to abide with him. It was a message he shouted with triumph.

Lift up your heads, O ye gates; and be ye lift up, ye everlasting doors; and the King of glory shall come in. Who is this King of glory? The Lord strong and mighty, the Lord mighty in battle. Lift up your heads, O ye gates; even lift them up ye everlasting doors; and the King of glory shall come in. Who is this King of glory? The Lord of hosts, He is the King of glory... (Psalm 24:7-10).

Deep Calls Unto Deep

With keen awareness of the dealings of God and the longings of his own heart, the Psalmist cried out, in Psalm 42:7, "Deep calleth unto deep at the noise of Thy waterspouts: all Thy waves and Thy billows are gone over me." Two deeps are mentioned here. The first deep refers to the depths of the human heart as it searches for the living God. It is a stirring from deep within. It comes from the unutterable and fathomless depths of the human heart. David prayed, "Search me, O God, and know my heart: try me, and know my thoughts" (Ps. 139:23).

The second deep refers to the depths of the heart of God as He responds back to man, "I have the answer you are seeking." This answer comes from the very depths of the heart of God, a depth we can never fully comprehend, "O Lord, how great are Thy works! and Thy thoughts are very deep" (Ps. 92:5). No wonder Paul wrote, "O the depth of the riches both of the wisdom and knowledge of God! how unsearchable are His judgments, and His ways past finding out! For who hath known the mind of the Lord? or who hath been His counsellor?" (Rom. 11:33-34)

A Craving to Be Filled

Following the reference to two deeps in Psalm 42, we have the interesting phrase, "at the noise of Thy waterspouts." What a picturesque description of the powerful dealings of God. A waterspout is a marvelous phenomena in nature that occurs in the midst of the open sea. In a waterspout, a funnel-shaped cloud descends to the surface of the water.

Rapid updrafts within the cloud cause an inflow of moist low-level air to spiral faster and faster toward the updraft region. If it were to be observed from its depths, it would appear to resemble a whirlwind. As the waterspout spirals upward, a mass of ocean water is also whirled up into the air, creating a powerful vacuum within its center. In response to this great suction, more water and wind rush in and fill the vacuum.

What is the psalmist describing here? He was describing times of visitation when the Holy Spirit came even as a waterspout. The psalmist knew the providential dealings of God, and he recognized the times God allowed great personal upheaval in order to bring to the surface things deeply embedded in his life that needed to be removed. What about the time David sinned and conceived a child with Bathsheba, the wife of another man? He thought he could cover up his sin. But God sent His prophet to bring to the surface what David had deeply hidden. God allowed great personal upheaval through the death of that small child. Yet through every experience, David recognized the ways of God. He sensed the deep vacuum caused by God's waterspout. He knew that it was the mercy of God that was bringing about collapse of his own sinful ways. His own pursuits left him hollow and empty. And worst of all, he knew the devastation he felt apart from God's presence.

The emptiness he experienced apart from the manifest presence of God caused him to cry out for the living God. In repentance he cried, "Cast me not away from Thy presence; and take not Thy holy spirit from me. Restore unto me the joy of Thy salvation; and uphold me with Thy free spirit" (Ps. 51:11-12). It was a desperate cry—a cry for the Holy Spirit to come and restore him and bring meaning and purpose to his life. It was a cry to be fully and intimately filled and connected with God. David realized that nothing else in life mattered unless he found his place in God. And as David cried out for God, so too the nation of Israel cried out for the living God.

Deep Calleth Unto Deep[2]
By
Rev. John Wright Follette

Down in the depth of my nature
Where the issues of life are born.
From the unknown mystical realm
Surviving through ages of storm.
A call is forever rising—
But its language I cannot speak.
It was born ere I had being.
'Tis the call of deep unto deep.

---

2. John Wright Follette, *Broken Bread* (Springfield: Gospel Publishing House, 1957), p. 124

Our mother tongue here is awkward,
For no words can fully express
The needs in the depths of nature,
In bondage to sin and distress.
Our hearts in their depths sorely ache,
They hunger, they call, and they seek—
Then silently wait an answer
To the call of deep unto deep.

Down deep in the heart of our God.
In mystical regions sublime,
In the Godhead's holy council
Long before our world or our time,
An answer was fully prepared
Every pain, every ache to meet.
In Christ, God's only begotten,
Is answer to deep unto deep.

The Answer indeed was the Word,
The Word when expressed was the Son.
O language of God how profound!
In answer what more could be done?
The heart of our God is hungry,
His portion, His people to seek.
"I thirst," was cried by the Answer—
'Tis the call of deep unto deep.

I think it is important to mention here that not all "waterspout" experiences in our lives are the result of sin or disobedience. I remember an experience I had several years ago that I can only attribute to

God's "waterspout." A friend of mine had just come through a very difficult trial. As she described how God met her need through prevailing prayer the glory of God was all over her. Suddenly something was stirred within me as well. I felt an intense upheaval in my life and craving for God at the same time. It was beyond anything I had experienced before. I began to cry out to God from the very depths of my being. In God's presence, my own plans and purposes no longer mattered. I only desired more of Him in my life. God had allowed someone else's encounter to stir my heart with holy jealousy. I felt a vacuum in my life. Only more of God could satisfy the longing within my heart. In response to my cry, the Holy Ghost came and gloriously filled me, satisfying my heart with Himself. The work that God accomplished in my life at that time remains to this day. God's waterspouts are worth receiving!

Perhaps this chapter has reminded you of your own thirst for God. You long for God to satisfy your heart, but somehow you wonder, "Is this really for me?" Be encouraged as you remind yourself of God's precious promises. From Genesis to Revelation, we see God calling to man. It was God who first reached out and thirsted for man. Way back in the garden of Eden, God called to Adam, "Adam, where art thou?" (see Gen. 3:9b) Later, in response to man's cry for God, He declared, "...I will pour water upon him that is thirsty, and floods upon the dry ground" (Is. 44:3a). His gracious invitation is extended to everyone who thirsts for Him. Hear and believe that this call is for you.

Ho, everyone that thirsteth, come ye to the waters, and he that hath no money; come ye, buy, and eat; yea, come, buy wine and milk without money and without price. Wherefore do ye spend money for that which is not bread? and your labour for that which satisfieth not? hearken diligently unto Me, and eat ye that which is good, and let your soul delight itself in fatness (Isaiah 55:1-2).

God longs to satisfy your heart. His desire to fulfill and satisfy your heart began with creation and will continue until the end of the age. Notice that one of His final promises in the Book of Revelation is, "I will give unto him that is athirst of the fountain of water of life freely" (Rev. 21:6b; see also Rev. 22:17). Open your heart to receive all that God has for your life.

A Lifestyle of Walking With God

David's awareness of God's presence was richly cultivated through the years as he walked with God. Let us note some of the many ways in which David made room for God:

- When making decisions, he sought direction from the Lord (2 Sam. 2:1).

- When he became ruler over Israel, he recognized the Lord's hand in establishing him as king (2 Sam. 5:12).

- As the ark of God was brought up from the house of Obed-Edom to the City of David, he danced in worship before the Lord with all his might (2 Sam. 6:14).

- When Nathan the prophet revealed to him God's plan to establish his kingdom forever, David went and sat before the Lord (2 Sam. 7:18).

- When his son who was conceived in sin with Bathsheba became ill, David fasted, prayed, and lay (repentant) before the Lord (2 Sam. 12:16).

- When the angel of the Lord meted out judgment upon Jerusalem because of David's sin, David acknowledged and accepted the responsibility of his actions in repentance before God (2 Sam. 24:17).

- As an expression of unfailing trust and a rejoicing heart, David sang unto the Lord (Ps. 13:6).

David's entire life was marked by his passion for God. Repeatedly in the Psalms we are given insights into this great man. He consistently called (18:3), cried (28:1), trusted (31:1), rejoiced (33:1), blessed (34:1), waited patiently (40:1), thirsted (42:2), boasted (52:1), walked (116:9), gave thanks (136:1), and spoke of the Lord (145:5).

The Joy of Restoration

David's efforts did not go unrewarded. He reaped the reward of answered prayer. In spite of all the difficulties that rose up against him, in each instance he called upon the Lord until there was full victory. Nothing less would do. With a grateful, rejoicing heart, he boldly declared, "Thou hast turned for me my mourning into dancing: Thou hast put off my sackcloth, and girded me with gladness; to the end that my glory may sing praise to Thee, and not be silent. O Lord my God, I will give thanks unto Thee forever" (Ps. 30:11-12). With simplicity and finality he was able to state, "...in Thy presence is the fulness of joy; at Thy right hand there are pleasures for evermore" (Ps. 16:11).

A Corporate Cry of Nation

Within the personal cry of David was also the corporate cry of a nation that had once tasted of the goodness of God and was, therefore, unable to find satisfaction anywhere else. Israel experienced great heartache in her wanderings away from God. The nation cycled in and out of counterfeit relationships, always to her own regret and degradation. She allowed gods of self-interest, gods of pleasure, and gods of worldliness and activity to clutter her way to reality. Yet the only cry that could bring the needed change was the cry for the living God.

What a glorious heritage we can each find in David. His cry echoed our cry. His quest for the living God articulates the cry we each struggle to express. His relationship with God invites us all to "taste and see that the Lord is good" (Ps. 34:8). God is the only source of lasting fulfillment and satisfaction, and He has promised to answer us as we call upon Him. May our thirst be quenched by the living water of our God. May His life flow through us to satisfy our own longing and that of the dry, thirsty land in which we live.

Heavenly Father, our hearts cry out for You. You alone are the living God, the One who can satisfy the thirst within our hearts. We know that You have placed this cry within us in order that we might seek Your face. Come by Your Holy Spirit and fill us. Remove those things that displease You, and give us a heart to follow You without compromise. Fill our hearts with a spirit of rejoicing that we might bless Your name in endless praise. Amen.

Personal Reflections

When we think of the cry of David and the emptiness he experienced apart from the presence of God, we can easily recall times when we, or others we know well, also experienced that same emptiness. We can vividly remember the upheaval of circumstances—times when everything we held dear was suddenly dislodged by events outside of our control.

- An upheaval of personal circumstances
- A face-to-face encounter with past mistakes
- An awareness of a vacuum within us
- A deep cry for God
- A longing for fulfillment and purpose
- A response from God
- A satisfaction beyond measure

Take Action—Record Your Personal Inventory

1. What experiences do you share with David?
2. List the causes you see responsible for these experiences in your life.
3. How would you describe your hunger for God?
4. When was the last time you experienced God's fullness? Describe.

Take Action—Look for Personal Healing

1. What situations in David's life drove him to want God above everything else?

2. Review David's prayer in Second Samuel 11 and Psalm 51. List some of the important principles it reveals for healing and restoration.

3. How can you pray for God to bring restoration in your life?

4. As you examine your spiritual condition and the way you are presently living, what changes do you think God would have you make?

Take Action—Become an Intercessor

1. Name other people you know who have experienced upheaval in their lives due to sin or disobedience.

2. How often do you pray for these needs and with what intensity? Describe.

3. In what ways did David's cry to God articulate the cry of our hearts?

4. Describe ways in which your prayers can articulate the needs of others.

Take Action—Reach Out and Help Others

1. In what ways could your victorious encounter with the living God serve as an encouragement

for others who also experience spiritual emptiness?

2. How can you share this message with others?

Chapter 8

Joseph: A Cry
for the Unveiled Christ

Then Joseph could not refrain himself before all them that stood by him; and he cried, Cause every man to go out from me. And there stood no man with him, while Joseph made himself known unto his brethren. And he wept aloud: and the Egyptians and the house of Pharaoh heard. And Joseph said unto his brethren, I am Joseph; doth my father yet live? And his brethren could not answer him; for they were troubled at his presence. And Joseph said unto his brethren, Come near to me, I pray you. And they came near. And he said, I am Joseph your brother, whom ye sold into Egypt. Now therefore be not grieved, nor angry with yourselves, that ye sold me hither: for God did send me before you to preserve life. For these two years hath the famine been in the land: and yet there are five years, in the which there shall neither be earing nor harvest. And God sent me before you to preserve you a posterity in the earth, and to save your lives by a great deliverance (Genesis 45:1-7).

> Likewise, in intercession, one may feel his heart consumed with passion over the plight of those for whom he supplicates, until God begins to reveal His own heart with an even greater love and passion for the lost.

Madame Jeanne Guyon is one of the best known women in Church history. Her writings have encouraged and influenced Christians for more than 300 years. Her works share the secret of knowing the unveiled Christ with simplicity and in utter abandonment to God. In one of her letters she wrote, "The only true and safe revelation is the internal revelation of the Lord Jesus Christ in the soul." Every man and woman who meets Christ does so on an individual basis. For each, the experience is unique and life changing. The following lyrics capture this truth very well.

What Jesus Is

To the artist, He is the one altogether lovely (Song 5:16).
To the architect, He is the chief cornerstone (1 Pet. 2:6).
To the astronomer, He is the sun of righteousness (Mal. 4:2).
To the banker, He is the bread of life (Jn. 6:35).

To the builder, He is the sure foundation (Is. 28:16).

To the carpenter, He is the door (Jn. 10:7).

To the doctor, He is the great physician (Jer. 8:22).

To the educator, He is the great teacher (Jn. 3:2).

To the engineer, He is the new and living way (Heb. 10:20).

To the farmer, He is the sower and the Lord of the harvest
(Lk. 10:2).

To the florist, He is the rose of Sharon (Song 2:1).

To the geologist, He is the rock of ages (1 Cor 10:4).

To the horticulturist, He is the true vine (Jn. 15:1).

To the judge, He is the only righteous judge of man
(2 Tim.4:8).

To the juror, He is the faithful and true witness (Rev. 3:14).

To the jeweler, He is the pearl of great price (Mt. 13:46).

To the lawyer, He is the counselor, lawgiver, and true advocate
(Is. 9:6).

To the newspaper man, He is tidings of great joy (Lk. 2:10).

To the oculist, He is the light of the eyes (Prov. 29:13).

To the philanthropist, He is the unspeakable gift (2 Cor. 9:15).

To the philosopher, He is the wisdom of God (1 Cor. 1:24).

To the preacher, He is the Word of God (Rev. 19:13).

To the sculptor, He is the living stone (1 Pet. 2:4).

To the servant, He is the good master (Mt. 23:8-10).

To the statesman, He is the desire of all nations (Hag. 2:7).

To the student, He is the incarnate truth (1 Jn. 5:6).

To the theologian, He is the author and finisher of our faith
(Heb. 12:2).

To the toiler, He is the giver of rest (Mt. 11:28).

To the sinner, He is the Lamb of God who takes the sin of the
world away (Jn. 1:29).

To the Christian, He is the Son of the Living God, the Savior, the Redeemer, and the Loving Lord.

Author Unknown

The Cry of a Deliverer

In Genesis 45 we read the marvelous cry of Joseph as he stood before his brothers during their second visit to Egypt. Unable to restrain himself any longer, he unceremoniously revealed himself to his brothers who had not recognized him. At least 20 years had gone by since Joseph had seen his brothers. In the intervening years, Joseph had served for 11 years as an Egyptian slave and spent two years in prison for a crime he did not commit.

Hated by His Brothers

From his youth, Joseph was a person of great integrity and had a heart for God. His unwavering confidence in the Lord kept him through the difficult times he faced throughout his life. However, Joseph was also the object of his brothers' hatred. His brothers resented the favoritism their father openly expressed to Joseph.

Now Israel loved Joseph more than all his children, because he was the son of his old age: and he made him a coat of many colours. And when his brethren saw that their father loved him more than all his brethren,

*they hated him, and could not speak peace-
ably unto him* (Genesis 37:3-4).

If their father's favoritism wasn't enough to make
Joseph's brothers hate him, his relationship with
them was further tested and strained by his dreams.
In his immaturity, Joseph demonstrated a boastful
attitude. He bragged about his dreams of future
leadership. He vividly described scenes in which his
entire family bowed to his rule.

When the opportunity presented itself, the
brothers devised a plan to make their father believe
Joseph was dead. They stripped Joseph of his
beautiful coat and then sold him as a slave to the
Ishmaelite traders on their way to Egypt. No one ever
expected to hear from Joseph again. But God was at
work, and He had a great plan.

The Providence of God

God's divine favor enabled Joseph to endure the
many hardships of his years apart from his family.
The spirit of wisdom and revelation operated so
strongly in Joseph that at God's appointed time, he
was able to interpret Pharaoh's dreams and warn him
of what God was about to do. Joseph described
seven years of plenty and seven years of famine.
Then, he gave Pharaoh direction for the nation. From
a place of imprisonment and obscurity, Joseph was
promoted to a place of rulership and prominence.

Because Egypt had food while all its neighboring countries experienced famine, Joseph's brothers traveled from Canaan to buy provisions for their families. Upon seeing his brothers, Joseph proceeded with caution. During their first visit to Egypt to buy corn, Joseph recognized his brothers but chose not to reveal himself. It was important for him to ascertain whether or not they had changed over the years. He also wanted details about his family. Now some months later, his brothers were in need of more food and returned to Egypt. It was during this second visit that Joseph revealed his identity.

Integrity Breaks Barriers

When the brothers came to Egypt on their first visit to buy corn, they left their youngest brother Benjamin at home with their father. Joseph longed to see his brother Benjamin, his only full brother (they shared the same mother and father). Therefore, Joseph devised a plan. He retained Simeon as hostage as the brothers left to return home, stipulating the conditions in which the brothers could return for more food, which included bringing Benjamin back with them.

The famine continued, and Jacob again asked his sons to travel to Egypt to buy more food.

So when they had eaten all the grain they had brought from Egypt, their father said to them,

"Go back and buy us a little more food" (Gen. 43:2 NIV).

But Judah was quick to remind his father of Joseph's requirements.

But Judah said to him, "The man warned us solemnly, 'You will not see my face again unless your brother is with you.' If you will send our brother along with us, we will go down and buy for you. But if you will not send him, we will not go down, because the man said to us, 'You will not see my face again unless your brother is with you'" (Gen. 43:3-5 NIV).

Unwilling to lose Benjamin, the child of his old age and the son of his beloved wife Rachel, Jacob did not want to entertain the thought of sending Benjamin on the perilous journey to Egypt with his brothers. However, Judah prevailed with his father by offering to guarantee his brother's safety with his own life, "I will be surety for him; of my hand shalt thou require him: if I bring him not unto thee, and set him before thee, then let me bear the blame for ever" (Gen. 43:9).

When Joseph's brothers came before him a second time, this time with his brother Benjamin, Joseph entertained them royally and graciously in his own home, yet he still did not reveal his identity to them. However, his affection for Benjamin was so great he needed to leave the room so that he could weep in private. Throughout their meeting Joseph repeatedly dropped hints of who he was and of the restoration that would follow, but his brothers did not see it.

As the brothers prepared to depart for their homeland, Joseph again tested his brothers by telling them that Benjamin would be taken hostage, for it was in his sack that Joseph's silver cup was found. What follows is one of the most moving accounts in Scripture of a godly appeal: Judah stepped forward immediately to speak to Joseph. He bared his soul to Joseph and admitted that God had uncovered their guilt. As he pleaded for the release of Benjamin, he freely offered himself to remain as a slave instead of Benjamin. Judah could not bear the pain of bringing further sorrow to his father by not returning Benjamin to him. Judah had not given lip service to his father when he guaranteed the safe return of his brother Benjamin. But rather, he was prepared to fulfill his word, regardless of the personal cost.

When Judah presented himself to Joseph, offering to become his servant in exchange for the release of Benjamin, Joseph's heart melted and all barriers between Joseph and his brothers were broken. Joseph could no longer restrain himself, and he wept openly before his brothers as he revealed his true identity: "I am Joseph" (Gen. 45:4). Judah's integrity paved the way for Joseph's revelation.

Judah's statement to his father, "I will be surety for him," and Joseph's later response, "I am Joseph," provide us with marvelous principles of intercession. Judah by his words and actions demonstrated the *place* of intercession. Joseph by his response to his brothers demonstrated the *reward* of intercession. Let us take a closer look and note the principles of intercession found in this account.

The Place of Intercession

1. *An intercessor stands as a substitute for someone else.*

   Just like Judah pleaded on behalf of his brother Benjamin, a true intercessor will go before his Father's throne on behalf of those for whom he pleads for spiritual release.

2. *An intercessor will offer himself as a sacrifice for someone else.*

   Judah offered himself in exchange for his brother Benjamin without regard to personal hardship or cost. Likewise, a true intercessor will sacrifice many worldly comforts in order to see God bring salvation to those for whom he intercedes.

3. *An intercessor continues in the place of intercession until he receives a response and assurance.*

   Judah stood unrelentingly before Joseph on behalf of Benjamin until he received the answer to his petition. So too, a true intercessor will continue in the place of supplication until there is a response and an assurance from the Holy Spirit that his prayer was heard and is being answered.

The Reward of Intercession

1. *Intercession reveals the King's kinship.*

Until Judah stepped forward, he did not know the true identity of the ruler to whom he made petition. His intercession brought a tremendous revelation. He was pleading with his own brother. With intercession, there is a great revelation of our heavenly King's kinship. The intercessor begins to learn and understand the mystical union of Christ and His Church.

2. *Intercession reveals the King's kindness.*

Judah made a passionate plea to the ruler of Egypt for his brother Benjamin, but he had no idea of the passion that this same ruler also had for Benjamin. With great emotion, Joseph wept on his brother Benjamin's neck. Likewise, the intercessor may feel his heart consumed with passion over the plight of those for whom he petitions the Father until God begins to reveal His own heart, which is filled with an even greater love and passion for the lost.

3. *Intercession reveals the King's greater surety.*

As Judah listened to Joseph's response to his request, he discovered that Joseph was even a greater surety for the safety of Benjamin and the entire family. By the providence of God, Joseph was sent to Egypt in order that his brothers might be spared. As the intercessor gives himself completely to the work of intercession, he comes to know in greater measure the infinite sacrifice of the One who gave Himself for the world.

Personal Examples of Intercession

Let me digress for a moment and share a couple of personal incidents with you regarding the truths I have just presented. Several years ago when God first quickened these truths regarding the place of intercession and the reward of intercession, my heart was set ablaze. With the fire of God burning in my soul, I took these principles and preached them in a Sunday morning sermon. I will always remember what happened next.

As I was sharing on the power of intercession, I made the statement, "And so you weep for your loved one, your 'Benjamin.' As you intercede on his behalf, you present yourself as surety for him. With Judah you also cry, 'How shall I go up to my Father, and the lad be not with me?' But this morning God wants you to know that Benjamin's own Elder Brother, the Lord Jesus, weeps on Benjamin's shoulder. Listen to His words of comfort as He tells you that He has become an even greater surety, not only for your Benjamin, but for the world. His passion and love far outweigh the love you feel. It is His intercession on behalf of your loved one that brings release."

With that statement, cries of relief began to softly echo through the congregation. Overcome by the anointing of God that had descended in that moment, I leaned over the podium and also wept. What I did not know at that time, but soon discovered, was that a mother had been crying out to God along with her daughters that very week for her son named Benjamin. As he struggled with one major crisis after another, the praying family wondered if God heard their cry. In the Sunday evening service, the mother testified that God not only gave them the assurance that He heard their cry, but He had providentially called their son by his first name. The power of intercession moved the hand of God.

The second incident I want to share with you occurred in my own family. One Sunday evening we were returning home from church where we had heard the announcement that my son's best friend Joey was in the hospital and was very sick. My son Jason was 11 years old at the time. As we entered the house, Jason ran ahead of us to his room. Within minutes, I heard Jason cry out in agony. Thinking he was hurt, I rushed into his room to find out what was wrong. What I saw amazed me and taught me a great lesson about intercession.

Jason was in his room crying out to God on behalf of his friend Joey. As he prayed I heard him say, "Oh God, Joey is too frail to bear this pain. You can put his pain on my body. I'll bear it for him." Listening further, I heard Jason say, "Lord, I'll give up everything I own; I just want to see Joey healed." Not wanting to interfere with God's working through my son, I quietly stepped back out of Jason's room. Later, as I reflected on what I saw and heard, I realized that the Holy Spirit had sovereignly taught my son principles of intercession. Without previous instruction, Jason was offering himself as a substitute and was willing to sacrifice in order to see his friend healed. God was no respector of age that day. He heard Jason's prayer and Joey was healed!

Let the words of these truths thrill your heart and move you to prayer. Join your voice with others who have gone before us. With them may you also sing, "Teach me to pray Lord, teach me to pray: Thou art my pattern day unto day; Thou art my surety, now and for aye; Teach me to pray Lord, teach me to pray. Living in Thee, Lord, and Thou in me, constant abiding, this is my plea; Grant me Thy power, boundless and free, Power with men and power with Thee." [1]

---

1. Albert S. Reitz (Broadman Press, 1925).

A Longing for Relationship

As long as Joseph concealed his identity, there could be no meaningful relationship between Joseph and his brothers. But with the barriers broken, Joseph could plainly tell his brothers who he was and why God had sent him ahead of them. Without hesitation, he unfolded the plan of God before them. He had been sent to preserve their lives and those of their families (see Gen. 45:5). He was able to offer them full restoration of relationship (see Gen. 45:9, 14-15). He offered them full provision for their future needs and a new dwelling place of blessing and abundance (see Gen. 45:10-11).

Trained by God in the school of adversity, Joseph knew what it meant to be:

- Rejected before accepted (Gen. 37:4-5; 50:18)

- Envied before honored (Gen. 37:11; 41:43)

- Stripped before clothed (Gen. 37:23; 41:42)

- Cast down before exalted (Gen. 37:24; 41:42)

- A slave before a master (Gen. 37:28; 41:44)

- Imprisoned before ruling (Gen. 39:20; 41:41-42)

- Forgotten before well known (Gen. 40:23; 41:57)

The Cry of Our Elder Brother

Joseph's cry was also the cry of our Elder Brother Jesus Christ, the one we offended through our sin and wrongdoing. It is He who unveils Himself as our provider. When Joseph cried, "And God sent me before you to preserve you a posterity in the earth, and to save your lives by a great deliverance" (Gen. 45:7), he also spoke for the Son of God who later came and offered a more perfect deliverance.

Jesus, who did no wrong, was rejected and despised by His kinsmen. He was cast out. He was sold by one of His own disciples, who betrayed Him. Yet by divine appointment, He comes to all who have offended Him and offers full restoration. With a heart overflowing with the mercy of God, He has provided a dwelling place of plenty for us all. And He lovingly invites us to His Father's house. Like Joseph, Jesus will unfold the plan of God to each one without hesitation. To all who call upon Him He will reveal His true identity, preserve life, and bring restoration of broken relationship. He offers full provision for our future needs and a new dwelling place in Heaven.

How well the songwriter, in the words of the hymn, *The Unveiled Christ*, expressed this revelation of Christ to man and His place with the Father as our great intercessor. The full manifestation of who Jesus was and why He came was not fully revealed until He entered into His sufferings. There on the cross, embracing His pain, He openly demonstrated the plan of God to the world.

The Unveiled Christ[2]

Once our blessed Christ of beauty was veiled off from human view; But thro' suff'ring death and sorrow He has rent the veil in two.

Yes, He is with God, the Father, Interceding there for you; for He is the mighty conq'ror, Since He rent the veil in two.

O behold the man of sorrows, O behold Him in plain view, Lo! He is the mighty conq'ror, Since He rent the veil in two, Lo! He is the mighty conq'ror, Since He rent the veil in two.

In Luke 24:13-35 Jesus beautifully illustrates this same concept. Two disciples were traveling along the road from Jerusalem to Emmaus in a state of defeat and despair. The Messiah that they had hoped for had died, and with Him had died all their dreams for a future kingdom. Jesus drew near and began to walk with them, but they were kept from recognizing Him. He expounded the Scriptures to them, telling them how Christ had to first suffer before He could be glorified. With their hearts burning within them, they invited Jesus to their home. Once inside Jesus broke bread before them

2. N.B. Herrell, (Nazarene Publishing House, 1916, 1944).

and suddenly there was revelation. They recognized Him as their Master and risen Lord. What is Jesus teaching us through this example? It is the breaking that brings revelation.

So often we want to run from our pain and sorrow. But Jesus teaches us that in His Kingdom, pain and sorrow work for us. When our hearts and spirits are broken as bread before the world, there is not only a fresh revelation of Jesus in our lives but we also receive a life-giving substance we can share with others. This manifestation of Jesus through our brokenness produces hope for a dying world. The use of personal sufferings for intercession produces healing and restoration for others who also suffer.

Heavenly Father, our hearts cry out for more of Jesus. We long to see the unveiled Christ. His power manifested through us will touch and heal this sin-sick world. In Your sovereign wisdom You have ordained revelation through suffering and sorrow. And so, dear Lord, help us to embrace the things You bring our way. Help us to gain insight into Your love and mercy from each experience. We pray that as we extend Your forgiveness, we will see the mending of broken relationships. Amen.

Personal Reflections

Unlike the other individuals studied within this text, Joseph is a type of Christ. Therefore, his cry primarily points us to the cry of Jesus Christ as He unveils Himself as our blessed Redeemer. However, contained within the story of Joseph are powerful principles through which we too may bring restoration to our relationships.

As we examine our own experiences in light of God's Word, we may find at times that we are one of "Joseph's brothers." At other times we may be a "Joseph." As one of "Joseph's brothers," we can recall times when we have broken off relationships and caused pain and suffering to those who love us.

- Jealous of those who appear more successful
- Hating others without true cause
- Deliberately destroying meaningful relationships
- Promoting deception to cover one's deeds
- No significant remorse over wrongdoing
- Maintains daily lifestyle as if nothing happened
- No attempt at reconciliation

As "Joseph" we can recall times we have been victims of injustice enduring great personal pain.

- Wrongfully mistreated by those who should love us

- Wrongfully accused of acts we didn't commit
- Wrongfully imprisoned by circumstances outside of our control

Yet even in these situations, God's principles are clear in how we should respond to those who have wronged or hurt us, and we should seek to apply these principles to our lives.

Take Action—Record Your Personal Inventory

1. As you review the characteristics of a "Joseph's brother," what similar feelings have you also experienced?

2. What circumstances in your life caused these negative feelings and habits to develop?

3. As you review the characteristics of a "Joseph," what similar feelings have you also experienced?

4. What events do you consider responsible for these experiences?

Take Action—Look for Personal Healing

1. How did Joseph behave when he was mistreated?

2. List ways in which he consistently demonstrated godliness even in adversity.

3. Before God changes our circumstances, He often wants to change us. Describe areas in which God wants to bring change in your life.

4. Review the way Joseph made himself known to his brothers. Note his conciliatory words and loving actions (see Gen. 45). Describe things you can do to bring healing in your relationships.

Take Action—Become an Intercessor

1. Describe people you know who are either a "Joseph" or a "Joseph's brother."

2. Are you able to pray with the same concern for both the victim and the victimizer?

3. Realizing that Joseph's entire lifestyle was an example of intercession, how can you demonstrate Christ as the Great Intercessor in your life?

Take Action—Reach Out and Help Others

1. Gleaning principles from Joseph's example, what can you do to help bring restoration to others who are in broken relationships?

2. Where and how would you offer words of encouragement to those in need?

Chapter 9

Your Cry: What Should You Do as You Wait for God's Answer?

By Him therefore let us offer the sacrifices of praise to God continually, that is, the fruit of our lips giving thanks to His name (Hebrews 13:15).

The voice of joy, and the voice of gladness, the voice of the bridegroom, and the voice of the bride, the voice of them that shall say, Praise the Lord of hosts: for the Lord is good; for His mercy endureth for ever: and of them that shall bring the sacrifice of praise into the house of the Lord. For I will cause to return the captivity of the land, as at the first, saith the Lord (Jeremiah 33:11).

> The best thing one could do with his pain was offer it unto the Lord as a sacrifice of praise.

Nobody likes going through difficult circumstances. How we wish we could avoid them. God doesn't promise us a life free from trials, but He does show us the way to victory. In this book we have explored the creative outlet of intercession. We have seen the glorious pathway to victory that can open before us as we cry out to God for those who suffer as we do. We looked at Old Testament saints who changed their world because their cries to God embraced the cries of others.

Perhaps you still wonder, "I know God will bring me victory someday. But in the meantime, how do I deal with the pain and disappointment? To deny my pain makes me feel like a phony. To say I have victory while I'm still hurting is just as bad. What do I do?"

In this chapter we will explore specific ways God can help us as we wait for Him to answer the cries of our heart. First and foremost, we must keep our eyes focused on the victory that God has for us. Not only will this keep us steady and balanced, but it will also enable us to respond in a godly way to our struggle and pain. In fact, God Himself encourages us by His Word that He does have a plan of victory for our lives:

"For I know the plans I have for you," declares the Lord, "plans to prosper you and not to harm you, plans to give you hope and a future" (Jeremiah 29:11 NIV).

A couple of years ago when I was meditating on the thought, "How do I wait for God, and what are His plans for me?" God used a passage from the devotional book, *Streams in the Desert*, to speak encouragement to my heart and give me further insight into what to do while waiting for Him to answer the cries of my heart. Perhaps as you read these words, God will also speak to your heart and give you the help you need.

"Here is God's loving challenge to you and me today. He wants us to think of the deepest, highest, worthiest desire and longing of our hearts, something which perhaps was our desire for ourselves or for someone dear to us, yet which has been so long unfulfilled that we have looked upon it as only a lost desire, that which might have been but now cannot be, and so have given up hope of seeing it fulfilled in this life.

"That thing, if it is in line with what we know to be His expressed will (as a son to Abraham and Sarah was), God intends to do for us, even if we know that it is of such utter impossibility that we only laugh at the absurdity of anyone's supposing it could ever now come to pass. That thing God intends to do for us, if we will let Him."[1]

---

1. Mrs. Charles E. Cowman, *Streams in the Desert*, *Messages for the Morning Watch* (Grand Rapids, Zondervan, 1965), pp. 320-321.

The Sacrifice of Praise and Suffering

Gripped by these powerful words of encouragement, I was led to read Luke chapter 1. There I found further encouragement and secrets to victory while waiting for God's answers. This passage clearly illustrated to me that God brings victory to those who offer the sacrifice of praise to Him even when their circumstances offer no hope or possibility of change. As I meditated on Luke's passage, I saw Zechariah and Elizabeth in a new light. Here were two people who were righteous and faithful before the Lord, and yet they struggled with a sense of personal unfulfillment. They had no children because Elizabeth was barren and now well advanced in age. But none of these problems stopped Zechariah from continuing to do what God called him to do.

I then realized the secret to their victory. Zechariah knew the place of the sacrifice of praise in spite of his personal circumstances. It was while Zechariah performed his duties as a high priest and offered incense in the temple that an angel of the Lord appeared to him to announce his prayer had been heard. Several things about his service in the temple caught my attention. First, as a priest Zechariah placed the needs of others before his own need. In his office as a priest, he was an intercessor on behalf of the congregation of Israel. Second, the angelic visit came at the time the incense was offered. What was it about the incense that brought such supernatural manifestation? Incense represented worship and praise to God. I thought about the Old Testament priests waving the golden censers filled with incense. No doubt the temple became filled with smoke as this holy offering was waved before the Lord (see Lev. 16:12-13). There, in the manifest presence of God, each person lost his own identity and God was glorified.

As I continued to meditate on the importance of incense and how it related to the sacrifice of praise, I thought about the ingredients from which the incense was made. Its very composition was considered sacred by the Jews. The four substances within the incense were stacte, onycha, galbanum, and pure frankincense (see Ex. 30:34-35). What I found out about these ingredients further heightened my interest. The stacte was a highly perfumed gum resin exuded by the incised bark of the storax tree. The onycha was a resin with a fragrant odor that was produced late in the year by specific stems and leaves. The gum resin called galbanum was excreted from the incised lower part of the stem. Burning the hardened tears of this resin produced a pungent and pleasant odor. Frankincense was a clear yellow resin that exuded from the incisions made in the bark of the frankincense tree.

The four ingredients of the incense, the gum resin, bark, stems, and leaves, were all ingredients from plants and trees. Each can be used to represent areas of our Christian experience. The gum and the resin came from within the tree. In order to obtain this substance, one needed to cut into the tree. It was so clear: *Pain and suffering were a necessary part of true worship.* There was no getting around it. The best thing one could do with his pain was offer it unto the Lord as a sacrifice of praise. This was not because an individual relied on his feelings but because God alone is worthy of every form of praise.

Even after this revelation, my mind questioned, "What should someone do if he continues to experience difficulty even though he has tried to worship God in the midst of his cry?" At that point the remaining ingredients took on new significance. I thought about the bark, the outer covering of the tree. It represented God's power to protect and to keep. You too may find it difficult to praise God when you are hurting. In times like these, it helps to fill your heart with praise to God for all His past blessings in your life. Think of all the times God met a need in your life. Remind yourself of God's providential care for you. As you do this, your heart will be lifted into God's presence.

Finally, my thoughts turned to the stems and the leaves, the foundation and the glory of our faith. My heart was thrilled as I considered unmoveable truths, those that shall stand no matter what befalls us. I remembered the precious blood of Jesus that made atonement for us and paved the way for our relationship to God. I reflected upon the beauty of a transformed life. Nothing can compare with the glory surrounding someone who has been changed by the power of God. These are things for which we can each be thankful. So in the midst of your cry, you may always offer unto God the sacrifice of praise.

The psalmist David also understood the importance of offering the incense unto the Lord during times of difficulty and struggle. He declared, "Let my prayer be set forth before Thee as incense; and the lifting up of my hands as the evening sacrifice. Set a watch, O Lord, before my mouth; keep the door of my lips" (Ps. 141:2-3). See how carefully he guarded his mouth from words of complaint. By so doing he found the secret of true worship.

Perhaps one of the most interesting things that caught my attention during my meditation on Luke 1 was the fact that God came to Zechariah when he had least expected an answer. He had given up hope of becoming a father long before. He had stopped praying for a child. He just assumed this was one cry that God would not answer. In fact, he was shocked at the angelic visit. When the angel told him his prayer was heard and his wife Elizabeth would have a child, he doubted and asked for proof. Although Zechariah may have forgotten his own cry, God had not. The offering of incense to the Lord paved the way for God to move on his behalf.

God used these truths to quicken my spirit and encourage me to believe that He would answer the cries of my heart. He also affirmed them to me in a very personal way at a time when I least expected. One Wednesday evening I arrived home from work tired and exhausted. I laid down on the sofa hoping I would be able to do nothing that evening but rest. However, my son, who was 12 years old at the time, soon came in and tugged at my arm, begging me to take him to the evening prayer meeting at church. I responded that I was too tired to go out, and that we would stay home that night. However, my son would not take "no" for an answer. He persisted, begging me to take him until I became ashamed of my behavior. I thought to myself, "I should be overjoyed that this kid wants to pray. Tired or not, I must take him to the prayer meeting even if I fall asleep during prayer." I will never forget what happened that night.

As I was praying at the altar that evening, not thinking of anything in particular, I thought it proper to offer praise unto the Lord regardless of my weariness. Rather dutifully, I began to thank the Lord for His faithfulness in my life. Suddenly everything changed. The manifest presence of God came upon me. I forgot my weariness as glory filled my soul. I immediately had more energy than I'd had that morning when I'd first started the day. Then it happened. A prophetic anointing poured forth from within me. It was as if the oceans of God had been released through my being. God mightily spoke through me and to me at the same time. He said He had heard the cries of my heart and had come to answer me. His voice was clear and unmistakable. I was shocked by how specific His answer was. He had come with an answer when I least expected it.

When I finished praying, I looked for my son and wondered where he was. After all, I had gone to the prayer meeting that night because of his persistence. It was not long before I found my son; he was fast asleep on one of the pews. What a sense of humor God must have! I was the one who was too tired to go out. Instead, I was completely refreshed and restored in God's presence. My son, who refused to stay home and insisted that we go to the prayer meeting, fell asleep. As I reflected on how God met me that night and spoke so mightily, I realized that the offering of incense through the sacrifice of praise had paved the way for God to move in my life.

Be encouraged, dear reader, that God has answers for you also. He hears the cry of your heart and longs to bring you the answer. Keep your eyes fixed on His good purpose for your life. See by faith the full provision He has made for you. No matter how difficult it is, let your waiting time be filled with the sacrifices of praise. Encourage yourself in the Lord.

He is faithful. He will perform His Word in your life. Find the place of perfect abiding in Him. Let your soul rest in His presence. Be confident, for He will be faithful to His Word. Be silent and let God speak to your heart. As the Holy Spirit deals with you, yield to His promptings. He is drawing you unto Himself. Most importantly, do not let any desire stand in the way of your relationship with Him. Be willing and enter into a place where you desire nothing but Him. As you submit to God and His dealings with you, you will find His love enfolding you and drawing you closer to Himself.

A Light in the Darkness

Have you ever heard yourself cry, "Why the darkness? Why the night season?" We can receive further help from the Lord when we realize that not all dark experiences are the result of sin. Rather, in His providence, God can allow the darkness to serve as a backdrop through which He will reveal with greater clarity the contrast of His glory. Perhaps you ask, "How does this work for His greater glory when all I can see is blackness?" Let me share a couple of incidents God used in my life to answer these very questions.

One incident took place when I was a young child. I had placed a ring on my finger that was too small for me. Consequently, it became stuck on my hand. After several vigorous attempts to remove the ring with soap, water, and hand lotion had failed my father took me to a jeweler to have the ring removed. I trembled in fear as the jeweler cut the ring off my finger with his big instrument. Once relieved from my distress, my natural curiosity was restored to full form. As I looked at the diamonds in the jeweler's window, I made what I thought was a remarkable discovery—all his diamonds were displayed on trays covered with black velvet. I asked the jeweler, "Why do you use black velvet?" He then explained that in order to display the full brilliance and beauty of the stones, it was necessary to use the contrast of the black fabric. Without this dramatic contrast much of their beauty remains concealed.

When I remembered this incident, years later I realized that God also has diamonds He wants to show off to the world. His diamonds are His precious people. He displays the beauty of His glory when He allows His choice saints to experience places of darkness. In these times of difficulty the glory of the Lord becomes brilliantly reflected in a people who remain steadfast and confident in Him regardless of their circumstances. We, His Church, are on display to the world, and we reflect the beauty of Jesus to those around us.

Another way God wants to help us as we wait for Him, is to realize that He is always there holding our hand, even when we cannot see Him. We never stand alone. The following incident took place a couple of years ago during one of my trips to the Bronx Zoo. Making my way from one building exhibit to another, I came to a building called *The World of Darkness*. This building houses nocturnal animals. Without the darkness of this building it would not be possible to observe these animals because they are usually asleep during daylight hours. There are signs posted at the entrance of the building warning you about the upcoming darkness.

On this occasion I happened to enter the building behind a large family of Hassidic Jews. Right in front of me stood a mother, father, and their eight children. I smiled when I heard the children sweetly call their daddy, "Abba." Within several feet of the building's entrance, we were surrounded by complete darkness. The only light in the building came from very dim lights inside the animals' cages. Suddenly panic struck one of the little boys. He cried out, "Abba, I can't see you in the darkness!" With a calm, assuring voice, I heard his abba say, "Son, take my hand. I am right here with you even though you cannot see me." I knew in that moment I had heard from God.

I thought of all the times I also have cried out in panic to my Abba because I could not see Him in the darkness. Through allowing me to witness this incident, my Abba wanted me to understand that He too was right there beside me even though I could not see Him. Why did God allow the darkness? Well, there are times when God will allow darkness, not because of sin or disobedience, but because what He has to reveal to us can only be seen through the contrast of darkness.

Embrace Your Mission

Finally, as you wait for God to bring release, view your cry as a God-given mission—a call to intercession. Take each difficulty God allows to come across your path and use it as an opportunity to pray for others who share your needs. Let your pain work for you. Through your suffering, you will be able to identify with others who suffer. As you cry, you will be able to cry for those in similar circumstances. Determine to see the purposes of God fulfilled through you. You are the instrument of God. Rejoice that you have been counted worthy to share in the sufferings of Christ. Also rejoice in the work that God is accomplishing in and through you. Remind yourself that God keeps His promises. He will not fail. As you are faithful before Him, the glory of His light will break upon you and your heart will rejoice in the Lord. You will see God answer the cry of your heart, and through your suffering and intercession you will also see that God has answered the cries of those you represented.

Personal Reflections

As we examine our hearts and the different circumstances we have been through and are still going through, we can easily wonder what we should do as we wait for God's answer. We have questions such as the following:

- How do I deal with disappointment and pain?

- Why does God wait to answer my needs?

- How do I remain stable under adversity?

- What will my future bring?

- What can I do to live in victory now?

- How can I praise the Lord when everything is going wrong?

- What does God want to reveal to my heart through these difficulties?

Take Action—Record Your Personal Inventory

1. As you review the above list, which of these questions have you also asked?

2. What events caused you to ask these questions?

3. How do you wait before the Lord for your answers?

4. What positive or negative results have you experienced from the stance you have taken?

Take Action—Look for Personal Healing

1. How did Zechariah put the needs of others before his own need?

2. Why was it significant that the angelic visit came at the time of incense?

3. Name the four ingredients used in the composition of the incense and give the significance to each.

4. Gleaning from the story of Zechariah and the victory God gave him, what course of action could you also take?

Take Action—Become an Intercessor

1. Name other people you know who share similar circumstances to your own.

2. Describe how you have prayed for their needs as well as your own needs.

3. Realizing that God works powerfully through praise and worship, how can you move God on behalf of yourself and others?

4. Study Isaiah chapter 6 and note how worship moved the hand of God in the prophet's life and brought a commissioning by God for service.

Take Action—Reach Out and Help Others

1. Describe how your victory while waiting for God's answers will bring hope to the Body of Christ.

2. In what ways and to whom can you demonstrate God's ultimate victory when you have received the answers for which you prayed?

Chapter 10

The Macedonian Cry:
Ministry Is Born

*And a vision appeared to Paul in the night;
there stood a man of Macedonia, and prayed
him, saying, Come over into Macedonia, and
help us. And after he had seen the vision, immediately we endeavoured to go into Macedonia, assuredly gathering that the Lord had
called us for to preach the gospel unto them*
(Acts 16:9-10).

> It is a cry from outside ourselves. But it is
> a cry that pierces our hearts and, once it
> enters, demands a response.

Throughout this book we have examined the
great exploits of God in power and restoration as
people surrendered their personal pain to Him and
allowed God to raise them up as intercessors on the
behalf of others who suffered as they once did. In
Chapter 1, we took note of the redemptive value of

suffering. We examined how God uses suffering to accomplish a great work of grace in our lives that could not have occurred any other way. We saw that, once it is submitted to the Lord, suffering becomes a vehicle for intercession rather than an instrument of destruction. We noticed how God brought corporate healing and restoration when individuals focused their prayers on what He could do through them rather than focus on the problems they endured.

In Chapter 2, we looked at Moses as a type of the nation he would one day lead. His hardships and suffering created in him a sensitivity to the needs of his people. He tasted on a personal level the injustices the Israelites experienced on a national level. As he responded to God's call, his life became filled with purpose and meaning. Through intercession and godly leadership, a people were preserved who had been slated for extinction.

As we examined Jonah in Chapter 3, we saw how the mercy of God reaches beyond the borders of our disobedience and failure. Within the cry of Jonah we heard God's longing to bring His people to a place of restoration. We saw in Jonah another person who was a type of the nation he would lead to repentance. His personal experiences brought him to a place of humility and dependence upon God. His suffering became the means by which a nation sentenced for destruction found the mercy of God.

In Chapter 4, we observed how sorrow motivated Nehemiah to become God's instrument of change. Sorrow alone could not rebuild the walls of Jerusalem. But intercession coupled with a plan of action became a mighty force that overcame every obstacle of the enemy. Through the work of Nehemiah and Ezra not only did God restore the physical protection of their city, but they also became restored in their relationship with Him and His ways.

As we looked at Esther in Chapter 5 we noticed the way a nation was preserved in response to a cry for salvation—even though no way of salvation seemed possible. Within the cry of Esther, we saw the cry for a new covenant. It was a prophetic cry for the whole Church of God. The salvation God brought to the Jews through Esther was a type of the salvation that God was to bring through Christ in spite of the law that doomed all sinners to death.

In Chapter 6, we looked at Hannah's cry. We examined the cry of the empty womb, the desire for fulfillment. We saw how Hannah's cry represented the cry of a nation that had become spiritually barren and lifeless. Having drifted from the purposes of God and His holiness, Israel was in need of a prophetic voice that would call them back to righteousness. On a broader scale, we noted that Hannah's cry is the cry of a barren Church. It is a cry for a move of God that will usher in His divine life and fulfill His purposes.

As we explored the cry of David in Chapter 7, we heard his yearning for the living God. Once again, his cry communicated the corporate cry of a nation who, having once tasted of the goodness of God, was unable to find satisfaction anywhere else.

The last biblical character we examined was Joseph. In Chapter 8 we highlighted Joseph's cry when he made himself known to his brothers. We saw in his cry and the cry of his brother Judah a revelation of true intercession and the principles by which an intercessor will plead for his cause. But more than that, we saw in Joseph a type of Christ and a revelation of His intercession on behalf of the world.

In Chapter 9, we explored specific ways we can receive help from the Lord as we wait for Him to answer the cry of our hearts, even when our hearts are burdened by pain. We looked at the practical aspects of offering our pain and suffering as a sacrifice to the Lord as a part of our worship.

I wish to close by turning our attention to the type of cry God brings our way to develop ministry in and through us. It is a cry from outside ourselves. It may represent a problem that we have never faced, yet it is still a cry that others cry. Once it pierces our hearts and finds entrance to our spirit, it demands a response. It is the Macedonian cry.

In this chapter I will share with you the details of one Macedonian cry and the ministry God raised up in response to that cry. It is called Barnabas Ministries, a ministry I have been privileged to observe from its inception. Its purpose is to provide encouragement to the servants of God. The story of this ministry began in 1987 when David Wyns, alone in the woods with God, had an encounter that changed his life.

In the stillness of God's presence, David heard the cries of persons who were *weak, wounded, and weary*. He heard the cries and "the groans of the dying rise from the city, and the souls of the wounded [as they cried] out for help..." (Job 24:12 NIV). The cries of persons who once had great potential for God and ministry, yet who were now wounded and helpless, pierced his heart. In this moment he realized that there are many people who once showed promise for ministry, which was evidenced by God's touch and anointing on their lives, but who somehow lost their way and became casualties instead of deliverers. How did these people in training for ministry fall through the cracks and be left broken and wounded, abandoned by the Body of Christ?

Confirmation of this new ministry was repeatedly manifested, even before its inception. Shortly after his experience in the woods, where God allowed the cries of other people's experiences and pain to enter his heart, David conducted a prayer seminar in New Jersey. He was teaching on prayer of petition, and he asked the group to pray for him without revealing the details of his burden. When the session ended, a man shook his hand, and in it placed a note and a check. Later David was surprised when he read the note and opened the check. The note said, "This is for your new ministry." The check was for $1000. Since there was no name for the ministry, the check was not made out to anyone's name.

The following Tuesday David taught a missions class. There he shared the testimony of the note and the check. When the class ended, another individual came up to him and matched the previous donation. He now had $2000. Soon churches became involved and other donations came in. With no ministry name and no solicitation for funds, God was providing for a ministry that would blossom beyond anything David or his wife could imagine. In fact, a vivid illustration of the fruits of the upcoming ministry was demonstrated during a trip the Wyns took to India. While there they received a large painting of fishermen pulling up nets filled to the point of breaking because of the size of the catch. The caption underneath the picture said, "Come over and help us."

Before David's encounter with God in the woods, he had served as missionary to Zimbabwe, Africa. More recently, however, he had been a Bible instructor at a Bible college. David was naturally interested in students with great potential for God and observed them regularly. Now, arrested by the Holy Spirit, his attention was drawn to heartbreaking realities. Many of the students who entered Bible school never made it to the ministry. In fact, many became sidetracked, losing touch with God's purposes for them and becoming heartbreaking statistics. Some of them fell into great bondages of the enemy through becoming victims of homosexuality, alcoholism, and spiritual indifference. "Where was the failure?" David asked himself. "Was there anything I could have said or done to adjust the statistics of these casualties?" The Macedonian cry had reached his heart. Too many people were not fulfilling God's purposes. The challenge came. David and Jeanne Wyns knew it was God's mission for them to help His people rise up once again.

In order to fully appreciate the impact of the new ministry God was about to launch through the Wyns, it is important to review a couple of details of events prior to their call. The Bible college at which David was employed had undergone a change in administration. With that change came reorganization, and the Wyns were asked to leave the school. In light of these developments, the Macedonian call recorded in the Book of Acts took on new significance.

Saint Paul and his companions had desired to enter into Bithynia for ministry, but the Spirit of God would not allow them to do so. The door they expected to enter had been closed to them. Had God's purposes for them abated? No. Instead, God saw in Paul the ability to respond to a greater cry. During the night Paul had a vision of a man who cried out, "Come over to Macedonia and help us." God was sovereignly moving David and Jeanne Wyns into a new path of ministry. Confident of God's dealings, they were able to say that they were no longer looking for reasons why their previous ministry had been stopped. The Spirit of God was calling them to a greater work.

The cry of the escalating failure of Bible school graduates took on new definition for the Wyns. With sharpened focus, God directed David and Jeanne to mission fields in Africa, Asia, and Latin America. There specific cries, which represented desperate needs, pounded at David's heart. Their cries became his constant cry. Barnabas Ministries was born in response to the cries he now received as his very own. His vision was to turn the mission field into a mission force.

With an ear to hear from God, Barnabas Ministries heard the cries of the weak. They were the cries of men in poverty, those who cried out to God for the simple tools of ministry. Since they were unable to equip themselves with teaching resources, the ministry responded by supplying basic tools such as (good) leather-bound Bibles, teaching tapes, and study books. Today the ministry has a mailing list of nearly 2,000 national pastors. National pastors receive additional help through teaching seminars that are conducted several times a year. These seminars are held throughout various countries across three continents by American pastors and Bible teachers willing to take their expertise and the fire of God burning in their hearts to other ministers abroad.

Another cry that entered the heart of David and Jeanne was the cry of the disillusioned—a cry David identified as the "cry of wounded spirits." It was the cry of nationals who longed to respond to the need and cries of their own people but somehow felt oppressed. Their potential for ministry was destroyed through lies of inferiority that spanned across generations. For too long they were told that they could not think for themselves and had nothing to offer. As a result, their wounded spirits prevented them from taking action to meet the needs around them. However, David saw their potential in God. He determined to teach them who they really were in God and show them how they could achieve their God-given potential. It was time these persons learned and experienced their real heritage—a heritage of victory.

Different regions presented different cries and different challenges. Another challenge that arose was the cry of the weary. These were servants of

God who had become battered and bruised on their journey. Too discouraged to go on, they needed someone who could help them get up again. As David and Jeanne looked at the weary, they saw the need for a "Mephibosheth" ministry. These wounded, hurting people needed to experience the kindness of God through the touch of others in His Body. By God's grace, the Wyns help lift these weary, battered servants to new levels in God. Restored and empowered by a fresh anointing, these same servants now minister more powerfully than ever before.

Through it all, David and Jeanne Wyns rejoice in God's marvelous provisions for their lives and ministry. They, with others who have joined them, are reaping a great harvest. Today, they see many nationals in places of ministry reaching beyond their own borders. Restored by the power of God, they preach the gospel message to places previously unreached for God.

Barnabas Ministries is holding forth the torch of hope, help, and healing to hurting people because someone heard a Macedonian cry and responded to the call "Come over and help us." With the compassion of God and the cries of strong intercession from His saints, people everywhere rejoice that their cry is a cry that God answers.

Record Your Personal Testimony

O give thanks unto the Lord, for He is good: for His mercy endureth for ever. Let the redeemed of the Lord say so, whom He hath redeemed from the hand of the enemy; and gathered them out of the lands, from the east, and from the west, from the north, and from the south. ... Oh that men would praise the Lord for His goodness, and for His wonderful works to the children of men! ... And let them sacrifice the sacrifices of thanksgiving, and declare His works with rejoicing (Psalm 107:1-3,15,22).

Have you ever taken the time to reflect all that God has done for you in response to your cry? If not, why not do it now. Your personal testimony is a powerful tool that God can use both in your life and in the lives of those with whom you share His goodness. Describe your cry. If possible, show how your cry relates to the cries of others. Then tell how you have prayed and in what ways God has met the need in your life.

If you would like to share your testimony telling of your cry and God's answers, I would be delighted to hear from you.

Concluding Remarks

In one pilot study conducted just prior to the publication of this book, I used this manuscript in its entirety as a text for a Bible study class in which 60 adults were enrolled.

We met together for several weeks, studying, praying, and working through each lesson. For our weekly assignments we prayerfully answered the questions and completed the exercises from each of the *Personal Reflections* sections. A healing process began. God's light penetrated darkened areas, bringing new understanding to many who suffered. God's love softened hearts hardened by pain and adversity. Every week dramatic results followed as lives were changed and healed by the power of God through the application of these truths.

We pray that you and your loved ones and friends will also find healing as you study and apply these principles.

About the Author

Rev. Rosemarie Brown is an ordained minister with the Assemblies of God. She has served the body of Christ for over 30 years as a Bible teacher, evangelist, conference and seminar speaker. She has become distinguished as an anointed Bible teacher with keen insight into biblical principles, bringing to her audiences a message of hope and restoration.

Rosemarie Brown is the Assistant Pastor at Van Nest Assembly of God in the Bronx. She is the Director and an Instructor at the Berean Bible Institute, at Van Nest Assembly.

Rosemarie received her Bible training at Northeast Bible College (now Valley Forge Christian College). She has a bachelor's degree in education from Roberts Wesleyan College in Rochester, New York and a master's degree from Lehman College in New York City.

She is married to David Brown and is the mother to one son, Jason Brown. Together they make their home in the Bronx.

To schedule meetings, seminars or retreats with Rosemarie Brown, please contact her at the following numbers and/or address.

Rosemarie Brown
c/o Van Nest Assembly of God
755 Rhinelander Avenue
Bronx, New York 10462
718 824-4067
Fax 718 239-0796

To order additional copies of this book, please contact the author at the above address.